Potential of a Man
vs. Truth

By Jenise R. McNair

Special thanks to Vickie Gould for being such an amazing
coach and inspiration.
Editing and formatting by Andrea McCurry
Cover designed by Monica Stanley
ISBN:978-1-7348331-1-9
Used with permission

Acknowledgements

To God, my Everything

Thank You for being the One who does not lie. Thank You for never leaving me nor forsaking me. Thank You for allowing me to fall, only to realize You were all that I needed to rise above. Thank You for using me as a vessel to show women across the world just how good You are and still allowing me to be my authentic self while doing so. You are so worthy to be praise and praise is what I will continue to give You! I'll forever give you all the Glory!

To my daughters, Jaylah and Jordyn

As a woman, I didn't always make the best decisions growing up. I didn't always do what was necessary to make sure I was okay. Instead, my focus was always on helping someone else. I made a lot of poor decisions; some of these decisions continue to affect you even today.

Despite all the hardships that I've been through, I took ownership and I've always held myself accountable. I'm sure people judge me based on my circumstances, especially being a single mother of three, but I never allowed that to stop me from going after what life had to offer. In fact, they only motivated me to push harder in life and to do the things that I once thought were impossible. When all odds were against me, I learned how to still come out with a win.

It's never easy being a woman in this world but I made a lot of decisions that made things even harder on me. As your mother, I never claimed to be perfect and for the most part I never painted a picture that wasn't real. My plan is to continue to raise you both as Queens, educating you on the ways of this world, preparing you for what's to come. And even when you fall short, because you will, you then will be able to look at me, understanding my story and knowing that no matter what, you will win.

You have complete control over your life and the people you choose to have in it. You two are beautifully and wonderfully made, better versions of myself. I pray as you get older, that you continue to water and nurture the seed that God has planted inside of you, blossoming into that beautiful flower you will become. Mommy loves the two of you with my whole heart and everything in me.

To my son, my first born, Jelani

I know decisions that I made tremendously affected you as a young boy and now as a young man. Growing up as a young black man is already hard enough, yet there are circumstances you still have to overcome with certain strikes set against you. With all that said, I've shown you what beating the odds looks like. I've shown you what hard work looks like. I've shown you that no matter what your circumstance may look like, you have the power to change anything pertaining to yourself and your life.

As your mother, I pray that you grow into the man that God called you to be, knowing who you are, and that you are loved. I pray that you always represent yourself in a manner that is respectable, honorable, and humble. I know you think I have been very hard on you while you were growing up, but it's only because I see potential in you that I know you can reach. I believe in you, and I want you to have the best and gain everything that's meant for you.

I thank you for being the best son a mother could ever ask for and I hope one day, you'll realize everything I do is with the intention to make you and your sisters proud. I promise to do all that I can to leave a legacy that you can continue to build on. I love you with my whole heart and everything inside of me.

To my Daddy, my earthly angel, and my MVP

I owe you so much it would take a lifetime to pay you back. Thank you, Daddy, for your unconditional love and support. Because of you, I persevered through so many storms in my life. Even though I brought three children into this world without being married, I am still able to walk with confidence, with my head held high, and enter a room with a commanding presence. I am able to represent myself in that manner because despite my poor decisions, as my father, you continued to love me, support me, and most importantly, you continued to build me up, showing me that my worth remained the same.

You filled my heart with so much unconditional love and I'm reminded every moment that you're right there rooting me on and supporting all of my dreams and aspirations. I want to thank you for who you are and everything you exemplify as a person. You've persevered through so much life-changing trauma and yet you never altered who you were. If anything, you became a better man. I know there's no perfect man out here but if one came close; it would definitely be you. I know I will never be able to pay you back for all you've done and for who you are but I promise to continue to make you proud as your Daughter. I love you, Daddy. You'll forever be my GOAT, my MVP, and the first man that chose to love me unconditionally.

To my sister, my best friend, my Olivia Pope Talia

When I was younger, I didn't realize how much of a valuable asset you would be in my life. I didn't know that at one point in my life, I would need you more than anything. Thank you for always being exactly what I needed you to be at the time, whether it was the voice of reason, the second mother to my children, or my very own personal accountant. On the days when life was just too unbearable to carry, thank you for reminding me that I needed to keep going, that better days were ahead, and that giving up at the time of weariness wasn't an option.

Most importantly, I want to thank you for loving my children unconditionally, for giving them what I couldn't, and for always having my back in any area that I may have lacked as a mother. I am everything that you're not but you possess everything that I needed to get to me to where I am today. I will forever owe you because I'll forever need you. You are the Best Big Sister a little sister could ever ask for. I love you forever and ever and even after that.

To my brother, my best friend, my hittah Daniel

I always grew up trying to be your female shadow. You always poured into my life mentally, spiritually, and physically. You always inspired me to think outside of the box and to definitely think BIG. If an idea didn't seem crazy at the time, that meant I wasn't thinking big enough. You always encouraged me to do whatever I put my mind to and to not stop until the task was done. You were the very first person to tell me, "Get comfortable with being uncomfortable if you want to be successful in anything." That mindset helped me to stay dedicated and committed to running marathons every year.

Most importantly, I want to thank you for leading me and guiding me spiritually. As my big brother, thank you for always speaking the Word to me and helping me find my purpose by seeking God first. Thank you for always wanting me to have God's best, even in my relationships. Thank you for also being the best uncle and being someone Jelani can look up to. You will forever be my second MVP because, you know Daddy comes first. You have been the Best Big Brother a little sister could ever ask for and I will continue to make you proud. I love you forever and ever and even after that.

To my sister-cousin Jeanarta

We've always grown up more than just cousins. You've always been there to first listen to me and never judge me. You were always there, making sure that no matter what, I was okay and no one messed with me. I could always trust that you would keep my secrets and comfort me in time of distress. You were always whatever I needed you to be in that moment. Growing up, you always were blamed for my mischievous behavior but the truth was you always just encouraged me to do what was right. I am truly thankful for you and the relationship we share. There's always loyalty, always love, and always support. You are the best big sister-cousin I could ever ask for and I am so grateful to have you in my life. I love you forever and always!

To my cousin, my son's Godfather Usama

I always admired the hard work, commitment, and dedication you displayed in sports and in school as we grew up together. You made playing sports and making straight A's look so easy. When you commit to anything you always give 110% and more. Choosing you to be Jelani's godfather was one of the best decisions I could've ever made; God knew we needed you. I can't thank you enough for loving and supporting him as your own. Even though you live out of state, that fact never once stopped you from making the trip to do pop-up visits to see him at school or making him do bear-crawls throughout the neighborhood. No matter what, you have always sacrificed and made him a priority in your life, even while being a father to your own children. I appreciate the morals, values, and work ethic you instilled in him. I pray Jelani never takes for granted, the man and father-figure you chose to be for him. Thank you for being there every step of the way to make sure he has all the tools needed to help him reach his full potential in life. I must say raising a boy as a single mother has definitely been a challenge but without you, I'm not sure I would've made it this far. I love you Cuz, I hope you know how thankful I am for you!

To my Framily, my Childhood Riders

Thank you for always pushing me forward and being my inspiration without even knowing you were. Each and every one of you has poured into my life, constantly reminding me that "The grind don't stop," and that "Our Dreams just can't be our Dreams and stay there." Thank you for always being there for me, even at the times I didn't know that I needed you. In the toughest and lowest points of my life, I could always count on you for a laugh or a good time that made me forget what I was going through.

Most importantly, thank you for your unconditional loyalty. Your loyalty outweighs your love for me and I wouldn't want it any other way. That's why I can say after more than 20 years, none of you has ever let me down or done anything to hurt me. I'll take loyalty over love any day.

I love each and every one you beyond any words that I could ever express. What I have in y'all, most people go a lifetime without. I was truly blessed when God placed each and every one of you in my life. Childhood sisters and brothers to the end! Let's continue to ride!

To my friend, my brother, my very own personal trainer Darron

At the lowest point of my life when I didn't believe in myself, you did. You were by side every step of the way in my journey to becoming a better version of myself. You helped me develop mental fortitude which makes me continue to go after the impossible. I can't thank you enough for the sacrifices you made to get me to where I am today, physically and mentally.

You caused me to dig deep, to push beyond the pain and work until I felt like I had nothing left. You changed my mindset toward working out and now, it is just a part of my lifestyle I can't live without. Everything I learned about how to push through while doing your crazy workouts, I can now apply to my everyday life. No matter how bad it feels or how much it hurts, I can hear you in my head saying, "You bet not stop!" My pastor said, "Your passion and your purpose will always be connected to someone else's need." Thank you for being so passionate about what you do and choosing to walk in your purpose. Because of that calling, you've helped change my life forever. I love you, Man, and I owe you. Thanks for being the Best Trainer Ever!

Special shout-out to my God-Kids Zaniya, T.J., and River and to my nephews Aaron, Amir, Cayden, and Crimson

Thank you for adding so much joy to my life. I plan to continue to make you all proud as well. I love you with my whole heart and everything in me.

Dedication

I dedicate this book to my Heavenly angel, my Queen, my late mother Joan. There isn't a day that goes by when I don't wish you were still here. But I've learned how to create happiness, even with the constant pain I feel from not having you here with me. Thank you, Mommy, for being an example of a virtuous woman, for loving God, and for taking care of your home and family. You loved your family so much that most of the time you forgot to take care of yourself first. I know I have fallen short many times but I promise that your legacy and all of your sacrifices will not be in vain. I will continue to be the woman you expected me to be and exemplify the strength that you showed me growing up. When people speak of me, I want them to know I am just a reflection of you. I love you, Mommy. Continue to look down over me and your grandchildren, as I know you do. I will continue evolving and becoming the woman you expected me to be, to make you proud. Continue to rest in Paradise, Queen. Until we see each other again, your legacy will live on.

Preface

Growing up, I was always known for my bubbly personality, a golden smile that would light up a room, and my positive energy that made me always ready for a good time. I was the friend that everyone went to for advice as the voice of reason, even at a young age. I grew up with two loving parents and two awesome siblings, who always spoiled me rotten because I was the youngest. I never thought that making "one choice" I believed was best for me and my family, would later cause so much turmoil in my life.

I was always taught, "All things are possible to those who believe," but on the flip side of that saying is the lesson, "All things are possible to those who believe they would never do this or never end up like that!" In a world full of possibilities, I never thought I would find myself in the lowest, darkest, scariest, and most painful place of my life.

How often do we choose to mask the pain that seems so unbearable, only to become numb to those hurts over time? Untreated wounds from my childhood caused my heart to be compromised one too many times all because I tried to heal myself with a band-aid.

As an adult, my attitude toward life never changed; I was still the same positive Jenise that people always expected me to be. But being silent about my childhood trauma only caused more heartache, pain, and strife. At the age of 23, I lost my mother to a rare disease. In the attempt to fill the void of losing the most important woman in my life, I entered into a very toxic relationship that I knew I had no business getting into. I subjected myself to domestic violence and emotional abuse, not realizing all of that yelling, cursing, and screaming at the top of my lungs caused such stress that I was diagnosed with a life-threatening heart condition.

I felt completely empty, lost, and scared for my life. Yet, I didn't leave the relationship right away because I still loved him. I finally realized that I couldn't continue to expose my children and myself to such abuse. I had to ask myself, whose life should I try to save, his or mine? I eventually left that toxic relationship for good with three young children, solely depending on me.

I struggled financially, trying to care for my children on my own. During the winter months we had to go without hot water because I couldn't afford my gas bill. I heated up water in the microwave just so that I could bathe my kids. The house was as low as 50 degrees so I put layers of clothes on my children, trying to keep them warm. I reached a really low point in my life when I realized I couldn't even afford to feed my children. There I was, hanging on by faith because I clearly couldn't feed them or keep them warm.

I smiled through the day to show my children everything was all right, only to cry uncontrollably at night because I couldn't believe this was where I was in my life. I thought to myself, "How did I ever allow my children to go through all of these circumstances that I never had to experience as a child?" I felt like a complete failure; I felt like there was no way out of this situation. If it wasn't for the fact that we lived in the house that I grew up in, my children and I would have been homeless.

My circumstance was so bad, I felt like God wouldn't even recognize my voice if I prayed. Before getting into a relationship with my daughters' father, I was focused on seeking God and trying to live a more righteous life. Then, once my mom passed and I entered that toxic relationship, living for God was no longer my top priority. That relationship came before everything and everybody. I put that dysfunctional relationship before myself, before my children, and even before God.

Oh, but it's so amazing how intentional God is and how He knew I would have to come back to Him. One day, while sitting on my bed and reflecting, I heard a voice in my head say, "He'll never leave you nor forsake you." I'd created a mess for myself but He led me out of it. Today, I am now an Entrepreneur, a Five-Time Marathoner, an Best-Selling Author, a Certified Life Coach, a Motivational Speaker and a loving mother of three. I now have the financial freedom to provide for my children and still travel across the world as I desire.

I chose to write this book so that I could help every woman who's drowning in their very own pain and sorrow. I want to put you in a position to own your truth and embrace everything you were, everything you are now, and everything you can become. I need women around the world to know, it doesn't matter what you are going through. You can overcome your circumstances and have the life you've always desired. You can become everything you are meant to be. You can achieve the unthinkable while doing the impossible. For every loss you experienced in life, there's a journey ahead that leads to nothing but WINS!

Introduction

Being a woman today is just hard; I mean extremely difficult. We deal with situations every day that can feel overbearing, especially when it comes to the men we date and the relationships we choose to be in. Many women just don't make good decisions when it comes to the men they select to allow in their lives. We subject ourselves to relationships that take us out of character. We settle for less than what we deserve and forget that our first priority should always be to love ourselves.

I believe we go about our everyday lives, operating in dysfunction because in today's time, we accept these problems and consider them to be normal. Fornication, abuse, toxicity, cheating, domestic violence, and chaos are all dysfunctions that the world has accepted. They appear to be normal when they take place in relationships that we choose. Unfortunately, most of these issues aren't discussed in church because many pastors and ministers would probably be frowned upon if they did. Anytime my pastor speaks on fornication or relationships, people get really uncomfortable and look as if he shouldn't speak about those issues in church. But these are the problems that most women, men and millennials struggle with. They stunt their personal growth and don't allow them to truly live up to their full potential. It isn't just single women who face these issues as far as experiencing cheating, being disrespected, or confronting abuse and dysfunction. Married women, unfortunately, deal with these same issues.

I admit that I am a sinner but I am also a believer and I know church isn't for perfect people. There's not one person who's perfect that walks this earth because it is extremely difficult to deal with temptations of the world and our flesh on a day-to-day basis. Fornication, abuse, toxicity, cheating, domestic violence, and chaos are all areas in our lives where we really need to be ministered to. Trying to figure out or fix these particular issues won't happen on our own. I honestly feel that these issues should be ministered to the congregation consistently and people should be more receptive when a pastor chooses to touch on these issues. Some of us women really need support and compassion when it comes to dating and the circumstances that cause us to make poor decisions.

I truly believe that people need to hold themselves accountable and be forced to evaluate what takes place in their lives when it comes to their happiness and what causes them to be dissatisfied. But instead, everywhere we look there's dysfunction and toxicity all around us. Reality tv shows, Netflix series, and social media, are all examples of entertainment we choose that are full of toxicity and dysfunction. Dysfunction isn't just something we deal with in our own lives; it has now become our form of entertainment as well. Instead of resisting the temptations of the world, we choose to accept dysfunction and chaos as our normality.

Women today are so preoccupied with trying to compete with the next woman that we fail to realize how we waste our time and energy instead focusing on ourselves and the areas we need to work on. But of course, it's much easier to point a finger at the next woman and talk about what she needs to work on instead. Women are quick to pass judgment on someone else's circumstances but in reality, they struggle and deal with issues of their own. When are

5

we going to start coming together, leaning on each other's strengths, and helping one another become stronger in areas where we are weak; especially when it comes to dealing with men and our relationships with them?

We pour our love into men and relationships that aren't capable of pouring into us or loving us back. Then we wonder why we feel unworthy and insecure. We can't continue to make poor decisions about our relationships because those choices affect our children, our health, and most importantly, our futures. We are bigger than our circumstances and we are stronger than what we appear to be. We misuse the tools that God has given us as women. It's time we use our tools to better ourselves.

This book isn't meant to condemn women or to judge anyone based on the decisions they've made that cause continual pain and chaos. Instead, this book gives insight to help each and every one of us learn how to accept our truth and walk in it, with our heads held high. Before I became a mother, the choices I made throughout my teenage years and as a young woman made a major impact on my life. Some decisions that I made caused my experience as a mother to be a lot tougher than someone who made different choices. Based on the circumstances of my life, I did not think through my decisions as seriously as I should have before becoming a mother. Of course, in the moment, we allow our flesh to drive us, so we make permanent decisions based on our temporary circumstances.

I just want to share with women across the world, that you aren't alone and that God already has a plan for each and every one of our lives. I have witnessed the impossible that God has done in my life and how he took the brokenness in me and made me whole again. I wrote this book because my heart's desire is to help women who may have chosen to put their happiness on the back burner for a man, someone they've loved or still love. My past is only a transparent testimony so you can understand that we all fall short and end up in compromising situations we never thought we would face.

We also need to understand that there isn't one good reason to allow someone to mistreat you, belittle you, or make you feel unworthy. As a mother of three, I had to endure and overcome a lot of circumstances in my life. But I will be honest, as a teenager, I used to be very judgmental about women in dysfunctional relationships or those who made decisions I thought were absolutely crazy. I didn't understand where they were coming from and I certainly did not understand what made them stay in a dysfunctional relationship. It's so easy to be judgmental when you aren't in that situation. It's so easy to say what you would and wouldn't do. But at the end of day, you aren't in that woman's shoes.

I've learned my lesson about being judgmental because everything I said I wouldn't endure with a man, I experienced. God allowed me to go through that process; He showed me when we make bad decisions concerning love and relationships, it just means we're battling with deeper issues that cause us to make those poor choices.

Women are nurturers at heart; we hope, we believe, and we only pay attention to what we want. Instead of focusing on the truth when we meet a man, we only focus on the potential of what that man could possibly be. We talk ourselves out of the truth, paying attention to only what we want to be different about that man, and thinking about how we will be able to change him in time. Of course, this choice causes us so many problems, heartaches, and unnecessary pain later on in the relationship. We must come to understand that Potential isn't Truth. Potential is based on what may or may not happen. It's time that we as women face our truth so we can finally live up to our full Potential, as well.

This book isn't about trying to find and keep a man. It's about finding and keeping yourself. But in order to care for yourself, you have to identify where the problems really lie and make the decision to finally walk in your truth.

Contents

The Vicious Cycle

Insanity: Doing the same thing over and over again and expecting different results.

— Albert Einstein

A vicious cycle is continuously making the same choices, ending up in the same place, operating in the same manner, giving you the same results every single time. How many times have you found yourself in the same exact place you were the year before? Going about your everyday life only to look up and realize you haven't moved forward and you're stuck right where you were before? How many times are you going to make the same mistakes before you actually pay attention and learn from them?

I don't think we really understand how easy it is to go about life, repeating that same vicious cycle over and over again. Maybe you wonder what this vicious cycle consists of. For starters, it means that we continue to deal with men in a particular manner, which clearly does not work in our favor. Do you remain in that toxic relationship that's not doing anything but bringing out the worst in you? How many times are you going to convince yourself that he will change and start treating you better? How many times will you keep taking him back, over and over again, only for him to not take you seriously and to continue disrespecting you. How many times are you going to look in the mirror, ignoring that voice in

10

your head that tells you to work on yourself but you're too busy focusing on trying to change your man for the better?

Trust me, I get it, Ladies. When we are in love, we give our all and so much more. We go above and beyond to fight for our relationship until we have nothing left to fight for. But the question we must ask ourselves is, "Are we really supposed to choose to love a man more than we choose to love ourselves?" We get so lost and wrapped up in a man, to the point that we become unrecognizable and lose sight of our own identities.

When we are in love, we have to admit that we do a little bit too much. We are Fast and Furious (doing drive-bys past their houses), Inspector Gadget (spying on their Facebook, Instagram, and social media pages), and IT (breaking into emails and phones trying to crack codes.) We are also actors (busting their car windows) or better yet replaying the scene of the movie *Baby Boy* as you tell him how much you hate him and how it's over, but then you turn right around and have sex with him. I know you're laughing because I'm laughing as I write this. We can be ridiculous at times. But when does all the madness come to an end? How long will we operate like this and continue all those crazy actions that we go out of our way to do?

How many times are you going to try to find a car he won't recognize because he's not answering the phone and now you feel like you have to do a drive by? How many times are you going to stalk his

Instagram or Facebook account, trying to see if he's cheating on you with another woman based off the comments that he left on someone's page? How many times are you going to get yourself all worked up because he sent a text to start an argument after you went out with your friends? Then you end up arguing with him all night so you can't enjoy yourself in the moment. Or better yet, pacing back and forth, screaming and yelling on the phone when no one is even listening to one another.

Seriously, why has this madness, this chaos, become our normality? Why is this craziness our definition of love? Why do we think this is how a healthy relationship is supposed to operate? Even if you know it's not healthy, why are you still in the relationship that depletes all of your time and energy? Why do we still date men who show no signs of making us a priority? Why do we still sleep with men who aren't committed to us, thinking that sex is going to make them want us more or speed up their decision-making process on whether or not they want to be in a committed relationship with us? Why do we still operate in the same manner, knowing those choices didn't work the last time? Why are you still sleeping with the father of your child when he already told you he doesn't want to be in a relationship anymore? Because you think you're going to get back together but he thinks the two of you are just having sex. That's it!

Remember, this is a no-judgment zone. Every situation that I mentioned is something I've done, except breaking windows or stalking his social media, but only because he wasn't on social media. I am guilty; I put my kids in the back of the car in the middle of the night just to drive and see if he was actually where he said he would be. I am guilty of allowing a man to call me all types of Bitches only for me to respond in the same manner calling him a Bitch ass nigga back. Yet, the very next day, we professed how much we loved each other, as if we didn't just disrespect each other the previous day.

I started to become a product of the environment I allowed myself to be in. I conformed to his ways, forgetting the type woman I was or wanted to be. My desire to try and change him only changed me for the worse throughout the five years we were together. The relationship was so toxic, yet time and my love for him only made me want to fight for us no matter what. When you invest so much of yourself into a man, you never want to just give up.

Trying to change and make him better became my first priority and I just didn't feel like I could give up on him or us. But once I had children, I finally realized what I fought for wasn't worth breaking my kids in the process. I allowed my children to hear us arguing, cursing, and my son even saw him push me once. As a mother, my desires weren't more important than my children's needs. What we had together was toxic but it was our normality. I stayed for the potential I saw in him, hoping he one day would become the man I envisioned him to be.

As women when we love, we love hard. But when will we make the decision to love ourselves even harder? How many times must we try to convince ourselves of another reality than what really takes place in our lives? We have to stop this vicious cycle that we continue to repeat, year after year, relationship after relationship. Think about how much work, effort, and different methods that we come up with to try to catch these men in the act. We could be so much further along in life, if we actually took all that time and energy and invested into ourselves and our dreams.

There was a time when my daughters' father and I had a bad argument (just like so many of the senseless arguments we'd had before,) but this time was different. This time I allowed myself to stoop down to his level. It was normal for him to curse at me and call me names but I never operated like that with him. It reminded me of a time when I was younger. During the summer after my high-school graduation, I got into a fight with a girl, cursing, yelling, and acting crazy; I even got my brother involved in the situation. Once the fight was over, I realized I didn't like that part of me. I didn't like who I was when violence, disrespect, or anger was present. I just didn't feel right and I knew as a young lady I shouldn't have represented myself in the manner I showed in that moment. Even though I was defending myself, that side of me was a side I didn't like.

After that fight I vowed to myself that I would start to carry myself as a woman and to always respect myself. I ended up getting baptized on August 18, 2004, right before I left for college. Getting baptized was my way of cleansing my past and having a fresh start. From that day forward I never cursed or fought again. UNTIL the day my daughters' father and I got into that argument where I made a decision to stoop down to his level. That was it! I wasn't going to allow myself to be called Bitches, Hoes, and a stupid MotherFucka anymore, without reverting back to my old ways. I just couldn't take it anymore! I got tired of trying to be the bigger person. So that day, I retaliated back on his level, calling him a bitch-ass nigga and a stupid MotherFucka back. This retaliation only fueled his fire even more, which made the argument escalate further. When it was all said and done, we believed our relationship was over.

Two weeks went by and I just felt bad and uneasy about our argument and the part I played in it; especially cursing at him the way I did. I wasn't raised to speak like that to the people you love. My dad never spoke to my mother in that manner and I never spoke to my siblings that way, no matter how upset we were with each other. Cursing to communicate on any level wasn't what I was used to, so I just felt awful.

During that time, I did not speak to him and honestly, I missed him, despite all the disrespectful things he said to me. I still wanted to hold myself accountable on the part I played in the argument. So, I bought a card and wrote him a long letter to apologize for all the things I said that were disrespectful and how I chose to handle my temper. I tried to call him but he didn't answer. I wanted to give him the letter personally, mostly because I just missed him and wanted to see him. Even though he lived in a gated community, that doesn't ever stop a woman from getting in. I waited until another car entered the gate and I followed shortly after.

I put the card in his mailbox but as I was leaving, I saw his truck in someone else's driveway. I instantly felt startled, confused, and a little bit crazy. My woman's intuition was sure he was with another woman. I immediately called my childhood friend Camil, who is like a sister to me. I told her what I'd just seen and asked her what I should do. You know, we always call that one friend who's going to give us the 'go-ahead' to act crazy.

I walked up to the door of the house where his truck was parked and rang the doorbell. But no one answered. I called him but he didn't pick up. By this point, I felt like I was really losing my mind because I tried to figure out whose house he was visiting. We were together for almost a year before the break-up and he had never mentioned knowing anyone well enough to park his car outside their house. I didn't want to leave until I got some answers.

He had a truck that unlocked with a code. Even though we broke up two weeks earlier, I wanted to check and see if he changed his code. Here I was being IT, breaking in and trying to find answers. I thought I was losing my mind. My insides were a ball of emotion, the kind of knots you get in your stomach when something is wrong. I punched the code in and his truck unlocked. At first, I was just

16

going to just sit in my car and wait until he got back, but I decided I wanted to maintain some class.

I knew how much he loved the radio system in his car and he always used the remote. So guess what I did? I took his remote because I knew he would have to reach out to me to get it back. The ball of emotion inside of my stomach wasn't going to settle down until I knew that he wasn't with another woman. Just imagining that he was at another woman's house drove me completely insane. I knew if he had to call me, I could at least try and get some answers. I had something he wanted and he had something I wanted.

When he called about his remote, I immediately questioned him about whose house he was at. I didn't get an answer right away but he finally told me he was doing work for a family friend and they left to get some materials. When he came over to get the remote, he told me our relationship was really over. I was disappointed but realized I had to respect his decision. I've never been the type of woman to beg so I accepted the break-up.

Another two weeks went by and we did not communicate at all. I was heartbroken because I thought our relationship was really over this time. Going from seeing each other every day to not seeing each other at all was a shock to my heart. Then one night, out of nowhere he called me around one in the morning. Normally, when he called me that late, I got worried that something terrible had happened. Fearing the worst, I answered the phone. He told me about some trouble at a club with his cousins and how he was upset. He explained that all he could think about was me at the moment.

He also told me more information about the woman whose house his car was parked at and explained they were just "friends." He also expressed his regret about how he could have done things differently with our situation and admitted the areas where he was wrong. At that moment, I was glad he called. I missed him and obviously he missed me too. Dysfunction has no rules and clearly love doesn't either. I didn't know what hurt the most: being apart or being together! Just because we really missed each other, we picked up our relationship like everything was normal. But we never once found a solution to our problems at hand. I was too green to truly understand what that moment really meant or how dysfunctional our relationship really was. With my definition of love and his definition of love, we were like the blind leading the blind. There's never a dull moment in the vicious cycle!

Getting back together, however, was the start of the vicious cycle that caused me years of pain and anguish. We weren't broken up long but it was long enough for him to have encounters with multiple women. While I was heartbroken during our break, he was out running around with other women. I didn't think once about seeing another man but I learned the hard way that men are totally different when it comes to sex. For most women, sex is an emotional connection but a lot of men view sex as just an action with no emotional bond connected.

I couldn't be mad that he had encounters with other women while we were broken up. I later found out my woman's intuition was right about the woman's house he was parked at. The cycle of disrespect and the drama began when he expressed that he wanted to only be with me and that those other women didn't matter. But in reality, they did matter. He told me he stopped seeing other women once we reconciled but the truth was, he was living his best life and continuing to play the field.

That vicious cycle got vicious alright. It started to mess with me mentally and emotionally. I started to question my worth and compared myself to other women as if I wasn't good enough. Over time, I truly started to believe I wasn't worthy. I allowed myself to get into a relationship cycle that I couldn't get out of. I started to love that man more than I loved myself. Every minute of the day I tried to validate my love for him. I didn't even have any children with him at that time. I just really loved the man that much!!!

Despite his poor qualities, he showed me a side of him that made my heart melt. Even though he didn't always show that side of himself, knowing that side existed was enough for me to fight for the potential I saw. Whatever he was dealing with internally, caused me to not want to give up on him. When we were together, we were inseparable; we laughed, we danced, we watched movies, or we did absolutely nothing. Just being with each other was enough. The thought of going to work all day and not seeing each other was torture. So, he sometimes came to pick me up from my job after telling my boss something that wasn't true, just so we could be together. Holding on to his potential and all the good times we had is what made me continue to repeat the vicious cycle.

You see, in the vicious cycle, when it's good, it's good; but when it's bad, it's really bad. We kept chasing those good moments because we were inseparable and our sex chemistry was incredible. I didn't think there was another man out there that could make me feel the way he did sexually. I got the best sleep cuddling with him and falling asleep on his chest. I can't emphasize enough how much I loved that man. But now that I'm older I realize I was more consumed with his outward appearance rather than his inner appearance. Tall, handsome, light-brown eyes, muscular physique, nice smile, and he always smelled so good.

He was very protective, almost too protective and never let me pay for anything. He was the definition of an Alpha Male. But none of those qualities stopped him from mistreating me or made him love me the way I deserved to be loved. I got to the point when I started loving him more than I loved myself. I thought our lives were going to get better. I thought eventually he would realize how much I loved him and that would make some of his behavior change towards me. I really believed things were going to get better because that's what we do; as women, we hope and believe.

My ego get stroked and I bruise her. — J. Cole

20

If a couple hours went by without me answering the phone while I was working, he always implied that I was cheating. That accusation made me so angry because cheating on him was never an option for me, no matter how upset he made me. But he accused me of cheating quite often and I later realized it was his own guilt that made him feel that way.

One day, I went to get a pedicure and he told me to call him once I finished so we could meet. I called when I finished but of course he didn't answer, even though he always answered the phone if he wasn't at work. I kept calling for two hours straight and he still never picked up. Finally, he called me back and said he was "asleep." Something didn't feel right, but I ignored the suspicion for the moment.

A week later, he got in the shower and I seized the moment to crack the code to his phone. Bam! I found out that while he was supposedly "asleep," he had picked up a girl that he was seeing on the side and did who knows what in those two hours. I immediately confronted him, "So, that's why you be trippin' when I don't pick up the phone while I'm at work because I can be doing a lot in those two hours right? You know, cheating like you!"

Ladies, I have stories for days and most of our stories may sound just alike. He cheats. He gets caught. You leave him. He says he's sorry and won't do it again. You believe him. You take him back. He changes for maybe two weeks and then guess what? The same pattern happens all over again. The vicious cycle continues. I went through five whole years of this

21

fighting, arguing, abuse, cheating, and all kinds of dysfunction.

Another incident took place close to our one-year anniversary. On this particular day, I decided to be helpful and clean his room, when I found his camera. I turned on the camera and the first thing I saw was a naked woman in his bed. I instantly looked at the date to see if it happened while we were on a break. However, the picture was taken during a time we were together. As I went through the pictures, I found a whole photo shoot of her naked in his bed with a scarf on her head. She was clearly comfortable, like she had been there before. Pictures of her all in his sheets, wrapped up in his comforter, as if she owned the place.

I instantly became an angry, black, crazy woman! I felt enraged, demoralized, and heartbroken. The thought of my man being with another woman was painful but actually seeing photos was just torture that struck me to the heart. I ran downstairs and handed him the camera asking, "Who is this?" He looked at me like I was crazy and proceeded to view the photos. I could not believe the story this man told me. He clearly thought I was a freaking idiot because he tried to tell me the girl in the picture was someone his friend was talking to. He said that he allowed his friend to use "his room" because he didn't have anywhere to take her. By the way, his friend was in a committed relationship.

His story might have been believable if there were no pictures in HIS camera. I confronted his lies. "Let me guess, he borrowed *your* camera and left the pictures in *your* camera for you? What were you going to do? Get the pictures developed and send him his copies?" I continued to scream and yell as I thought about how he was sleeping with me and at the same time fooling around with her and whoever else he had in his black book. I thought to myself, "How much of a fool am I going to continue to be? How are his actions in any way remotely loving? How can I love this man more than I love myself when he clearly shows me my feelings mean nothing to him? How do I continue to allow this man to make me feel unworthy and not enough?" I realized we could no longer proceed like we were if this was what love was!

I told him I was done, that betrayal was the last straw for me. I couldn't take any more cheating; I had more than enough of the blatant disrespect. I reached a place where I realized I was settling for less than I knew I deserved. He treated me horribly and the only result of our relationship was to make me feel insecure about myself; to make me feel like I wasn't enough.

Two weeks passed but my feelings didn't change. I stuck to what I said; this time around I was really done. My cousin came to town for his football camp and he got a party bus for his friends to celebrate his success with the camp. That night I was so lit on that party bus, I don't know if I was celebrating my cousin's camp being successful or the fact that I was finally free from that toxic, dysfunctional, and abusive relationship.

My son's birthday party was the next day and my period was due, but it was disturbingly light. I instantly started to worry and said to myself, "I can't be pregnant!" I was confident that I wasn't because the last time we had sex I took a Plan-B pill. I knew our relationship was dysfunctional and I didn't want to bring a child into this world on those terms. Trust me, I wasn't trying to trap him, I knew exactly who and what I was dealing with. Having a baby wouldn't make him love me any more or make him treat me any better.

When the next month arrived, I realized I missed my period. Now, I don't miss my period unless I'm pregnant; I'm that woman! So, I took a pregnancy test, and yep, I was pregnant!!! There I was, looking at the pregnancy test with that knot in my stomach, thinking to myself, "Why would I want to bring a child into this world on these terms?" I know having a baby is supposed to be joyful but those weren't my feelings in the moment.

When I told him the news, he said, "Well, it's about time!!!"

I looked at him, confused. Thinking to myself, "Wait, were you trying to get me pregnant?"

He responded, "I got you, we are going to be okay."

I was shocked at his reaction to my pregnancy and I assumed when he said, "We are going to be okay," that meant he was going to change. Silly me. Being pregnant only meant one thing and one thing only: the vicious cycle continued but now, with a baby involved.

24

The vicious cycle was immediately taken up a couple of notches. Every time I went to his house and slept over, his bed reminded me of the woman in the photographs. Then I remembered all the other times he cheated. He instantly saw my face and assured me, "Those are new sheets," or, "I just got that comforter." We might be watching a movie when something reminded me that he cheated. He looked at me and said, "Are you having a moment?" I could only think about his inability to be faithful to me. He comforted me during those times to try and reassure me I was the only woman he wanted. So, I allowed myself to fight for a dysfunctional relationship that slowly ate at any happiness I had left inside of me. I knew I didn't belong in the relationship but I stayed, still holding onto hope. It seemed like the more I believed in him, the more he cheated and disrespected me.

Whatever is happening in your life that causes you unhappiness, only occurs because you choose to handle the situation in the same manner that you have tried before. You must accept and walk in your truth. This vicious cycle that we subject ourselves to becomes our normality when there's just nothing normal about it. And the reality about dealing with the vicious cycles is, a lot of married women go through this same vicious cycle but their situation is a lot deeper. They have a binding contract since they vowed 'for better or for worse,' that makes them feel like they *have* to continue to fight for their marriage. What is our excuse as single women when we aren't even married to these men? How we choose to let someone continually treat us will soon affect how we choose to treat ourselves.

Do you think that just because I had his child, his behavior got better? No, it only got worse. No matter how many times I left, having his child meant he still had access to me, which meant I started to fight for our relationship even more. I had to view him from a different lens. He was no longer just my boyfriend; he was also the father of my child. So, I really felt the need to stick it out and stay the course. I was no longer fighting for me and him, I started to fight for our family because family is very important to me.

Whatever you are going through that causes you to repeat the same vicious cycle, nothing is going to change until you change. You have to *want* to break that cycle. You have to *know* that making the same decisions is not going to give you different results. As long as you continue to handle your circumstances in the same manner that you always have, you will achieve the same results as you always have. The vicious cycles must end but that resolution has to start with you making a choice to do something different.

Change can only happen when change is a top priority for you. Don't allow the time you invested, other people's opinions, or fear stop you from breaking this vicious cycle. Your happiness and your health should be your only priority because there's absolutely nothing healthy about the vicious cycles we subject ourselves to. Whatever you feel you are fighting for won't be worth what you will lose in the process.

Remember, how you choose to treat yourself will always be the standard of how you'll allow others to treat you.

Her Truth

There's Beauty and Freedom beyond our pain.

— Jenise McNair

I grew up in a two-parent household, the youngest of three children. I was far from rich but was nowhere near poor either. I'd like to say we were a middle-class family. I didn't always get what I wanted but my parents always made sure I had what I needed. My parents were very loving; they truly sacrificed all that they could to give us a good life. I was raised with my father and my brother in the same household. I wouldn't trade either of them for the world. My father always treated me like a princess, giving me diamond rings, cards, candy on Valentine's Day and other special occasions. My father is the definition of what a man should be! Of course, that's just my opinion but there are many people who would agree.

When I found myself stuck in the vicious cycle, I had to ask myself, "How did I get here? How did I allow myself to get into a relationship where I am belittled and treated as less than what I deserve? How did I go my whole life ready to fight anyone who disrespected me but accepted a man who calls me a bitch every time he gets upset? How did I allow myself to be in a relationship with a man who doesn't value or respect me?"

Growing up, my father did his job raising me with love and building me up with confidence. But something going on within me allowed me to continue the vicious cycle. A lot of times the truth is associated with pain; but I've learned you truly can't conquer what you don't confront. There are many people in the world that suppress the pain caused by a childhood trauma. We allow ourselves to become numb to the pain overtime. Choosing to not deal with your pain can affect how you are as a parent. Sometimes the anger and the frustration from the pain you feel is taken out on your children in some way. How can we effectively love our children to our full capacity, if we don't choose to love ourselves first and heal. The memories that we run from only resurface throughout our lives, in every aspect of our lives. In order to fix a problem and prevent it from happening again, you must first find out how it happened and why it happened.

Walking in your truth means accepting the inevitable, accepting circumstances that have taken place in your life, and accepting things about yourself that you cannot change; embracing the good and bad about yourself. Walking in your truth is one of the hardest and most painful steps that you'll ever have to take; but it's the best gift you can ever give to yourself. Hitting rock bottom and not recognizing who I had become was devastating! I knew in order for me to get up and stay up, walking in my truth was the only way.

Without walking in your truth you'll never be your true authentic self. For so long, I masked the pain that I felt on the inside, always trying to be strong and smiling no matter how I felt. I had to make a choice to do something different because my pain only made matters worse for me. I held my problems in for 22 years, not knowing how much they affected my life or the decisions I made throughout the years. Unfortunately, I didn't realize you can't run from something that is a part of you.

Walking in your painful truths can be extremely hard, especially when someone else played a part in your pain. It is even more difficult when that person may not be ready to take ownership or accountability for the role they played. But their unwillingness is okay as long as you're ready to walk in your truth. Walking in your truth sets you free and it truly allows you to deal with what has taken place in your life, the aftermath of how it made you feel, and how it has affected you. Walking in your truth allows you to heal from the pain that seems unbearable at times. No one knows you better than you know yourself. Masking your pain often seems like the only solution to your problems. It's the easiest solution that we choose to use quite often. Sometimes we just need to sit back and ask ourselves, "What is really the problem?"

Why do we accept and settle for far less than what we deserve? Why do we continue to repeat the same vicious cycle? The initial problem may be the man who acts harshly and treats you like crap BUT what makes you stay and think you don't deserve more than he can give? I know you may not want to hear this advice, but at some point, Ladies, we have to face the deeper issues that cause us to choose men who don't act in our best interests.

My perspective on why women allow more BS than need be is that they have a low self-worth due to lack of affection, father neglect, weight issues, emotional eating, insecurities about appearance, rejection, sexual abuse, sexual abuse as a child, physical abuse, substance abuse or neglect by parents, being an orphan or in foster care, verbal abuse as a child, betrayal or just shameful circumstances that one experienced in the past. There are so many factors that can affect why we choose to allow someone to mistreat us. It's time as women, that we start focusing on who we are and the deep, inner issues that we battle which cause us to make poor decisions in our relationships. I know that remembering the past may open up some wounds that you chose to forget, but what good is that suppression doing for you?

You can't conquer what you don't confront! No matter what you've been through in your life or in your past, only you have control over your future. Anybody that put you down while you were growing up, whether parents, schoolmates, significant others, or anyone else, does not determine who you are or who you are meant to be. It's up to you to know your own self-worth. You're not who those people say you are, you are only who God says you are! There is a point in each woman's life when she falls short or makes poor decisions. Ladies, you have to understand that your past doesn't define you or your destiny. It doesn't define your worthiness or what you deserve in your life. In view of my own shortcomings, I had to learn that God loves me whole-heartedly and there's nothing I could ever do to make Him love me any less or deny me as His child. There were many times when I put others before Him, yet when everything went wrong, I reached out for His helping hand and He was right there to pick me up. We aren't perfect but God still loves us unconditionally.

I know there are situations you wish you could have done differently or circumstances you went through that you had no control over. But your life is just as precious as that of any other woman who may not have experienced what you went through or made the decisions you made. It is important for us as women to walk in our truth or the Devil will continue to make us feel ashamed, unworthy, and helpless. Whatever the problem is that causes you to settle for less than you deserve, it's time you finally deal with that issue head-on. We are often more willing to deal with the pain that will break us rather than deal with the pain that will mend us. In other words, we will continue to be with men who hurt us, belittle us, and disrespect us, causing us pain and breaking our spirits but we refuse to deal with the pain from our past so we can heal and become whole. I know walking in your truth and trying to heal correctly is easier said than done, so I'm going to be transparent with you.

Walking in your truth can be very painful at first, but as I began to walk in my truth, I had to acknowledge my poor decisions and the men I chose to be with. Most importantly, my truth was that I allowed a man to totally disrespect me and treat me like I was worthless! I was blessed enough to be raised with my father and my brother in the same household. But as I mentioned earlier, I held my truth in for 22 years, not knowing how much it affected my life and the decisions I made throughout the years.

Then, one Sunday I went to church and a guest pastor taught that morning on the subject of "Shame." Instantly, I felt he was talking to me! He said, sometimes we are shameful of situations that happened in our past that we had no control over. At that point, tears started welling up in my eyes. As he spoke, I realized a painful part of my truth was something I had no control over and yet it was something I never wanted to accept. I knew I had to confront my truth one day, but it was just easier for me to ignore my truth and go on with my life as if that part of my truth never existed.

I left church that morning and called my brother to come over so we could talk. The first thing he said was, "You're not about to tell me you're pregnant, are you?" I started laughing and replied, "No Fool, just come over." My big brother is my homie; he's like a brother and a best friend put together. When he came over, I proceeded to tell him my truth that I held in for 22 years. I looked at him, trying to hold back my tears, as I told him that I was molested when I was six years old by a family friend who was much older than me. Once I finally got the words out, I instantly started crying like I was that six-year-old little girl all over again, as if the incident had just happened. My brother hugged me tightly and started praying for my healing and my life.

I knew I needed to tell my dad because I felt that telling him would help start my healing process. But I didn't know how to inform my dad without making him question if he was a bad parent because I had been hurt. I lost my mom five years prior to that time so I never got a chance to tell her. My brother told me to pray about telling my father and that God would reveal when the time was right to mention what had happened to my dad.

Can you imagine holding in such pain for 22 years? I always wanted to tell my parents but I didn't want them to hurt knowing something like that happened to their baby girl. I never doubted that they would believe me if I told them, but I knew the news would cause drama because the perpetrator was a very close friend of the family. So, I made a decision as a six-year old to carry that burden of pain alone and I kept that incident to myself for 22 years. Once I was older, being molested didn't cause me to go out and sleep with a bunch of men because I wasn't looking for love. I didn't need any more love! I knew my parents loved me but as a little girl, I didn't understand why something like that had to happen to me. So, through the years, I held my truth in and never told anyone. God revealed the right time to tell my dad and he actually took it better than I anticipated.

As terrible as I thought being sexually molested was, I never thought anything else could hurt just as

33

much. But when my senior year of high school approached, something happened that completely devastated me and crushed my entire soul. I discovered that my father was unfaithful to my mother. I thought, "Not my daddy, my hero, not the one man who's never let me down!" I could no longer think clearly, focus in school, or play my best on the basketball court.

I didn't want to believe that my daddy could do something like that. I didn't want to accept that he was capable of making a choice that would hurt his wife and most of all his family. All my life, I perceived my dad to be a man who could do no wrong. Every 'daddy's girl' thinks highly about her dad, so the truth about my father crushed me. I was so furious, so distraught and disappointed, that I ended up packing my bags and leaving. I couldn't stand to look at my father or even be around him for more than two minutes. I ended up going to my childhood best friend's house where I stayed for about a month. I did what I knew best; I ran from a situation that I had no control over.

My mother allowed me to have my moment, but after a month or so, she called me and said it was time to come back home. Going back home meant I had to face my father and actually accept the fact that he wasn't perfect. It was a very painful truth that I just didn't want to accept. As a young teenager, I truly did not understand my mother's position. I couldn't understand why she didn't want to leave him, but she thought I was crazy when I suggested that idea.

She sat me down and had a talk with my sister and me, explaining how she played a role in his infidelity. Despite his poor decision, she made it very clear that he was a good man and she wasn't leaving him. That was the moment I realized that my father was still human and flawed. Yet his one mistake didn't outweigh the type of man he was to our family. He worked every day and willingly gave his entire paycheck to my mom. My dad was like a genie in a bottle; whatever my mother wanted - her wish was his command. My father was always a stand-up guy, an amazing father, and no matter what, his family always came *first*. Despite the hurt I felt, my father deserved my forgiveness, especially because I knew of all the disappointments I put him through. He never gave up on me, so as his daughter, I couldn't give up on him either.

After high school, I decided to go to cosmetology school in North Carolina. I worked in the evenings at Cracker Barrel to have extra spending money for myself, and that is where I met my son's father. Before cosmetology school, I'd only had one boyfriend who was my high school sweetheart. Trust me when I say, the vicious cycle probably started with my high-school sweetheart. I used to stress all my friends out when it came to dating him by complaining to them how he chose his friends over me. Girls are just so much more mature than boys as teenagers and we expect boys to really be able to know what they want and to carry themselves as if they are mature men. Having expectations in a high-school relationship was just as stressful, believe it or not. Even back then I put our relationship before myself.

I was too young to realize I should have focused more on my school work rather than trying to fight for a juvenile relationship. But at the time, I was hoping we would spend the rest of our lives together. But he did what any high school boy would do; he strung me along and stressed me out in the process. He was also in North Carolina for college, but was focused on himself. After a while, I got fed up with him giving me mixed signals and called upon myself to move on. We weren't in a relationship at the time but I was still waiting on him to figure out what he wanted to do when it came to us.

I became friends with my son's father at work and that friendship turned into more. Then, BAM! I ended up pregnant at 19! He was the second person I ever slept with and I ended up pregnant. My high-school sweetheart was pissed when I told him. Even though we weren't together, I believed there was still a possibility of us in the future so I felt that he should know about my pregnancy. I was always against abortions growing up, but I questioned myself and asked, "How can I have a baby with someone I've only known for four months?" A choice I didn't believe in, suddenly became an option.

As women, we are so quick to pass judgment when we aren't in someone else's shoes. I had just finished hair school, obtained my Cosmetologist license and attended Guilford College, trying to get my business degree. I took four morning classes, worked in a hair salon in the afternoons then worked at Cracker Barrel at night. Normally, people go to college first and then work, but I wanted to be able to make money while I was in college. I had big plans to get my degree and travel the world as a platform artist. I knew those plans would be completely altered if I decided to have a baby. Even though we weren't together at the time, my high school sweetheart was still my plan for the future so I knew my decision about keeping the baby would alter that relationship as well.

In my family, having a baby out of wedlock was frowned upon. I had so much pressure on me to live up to my siblings' standard since they both went to college and graduated with degrees. My son's father, who was a junior at North Carolina A&T, made it very clear that he wasn't ready to be a father. At the time, he felt as though getting the abortion was the best decision for us. I called my big sister and told her my situation; she did my dirty work and told both my parents the news. My mother fell out, crying and screaming, but my dad was cool, calm, and collected, as always. My dad told me when I was in high school, "If you ever get pregnant, I expect you to be a woman and take care of your responsibility." So, after my sister told him the news, he called me and said, "Hey, Baby Girl, your sister just told me the news. Remember what I used to tell you in high school? You still need to be responsible but I also will support you as your father in whatever decision you make."

Even though my dad gave me peace knowing he supported me, I couldn't help but to think about my

37

high-school sweetheart, my career, and the fact there was a chance my child would grow up without his father being around. I felt so confused and I didn't know what decision was truly best for me. I couldn't believe this situation was happening to me and I just didn't know what to do. I ended up making an appointment to have the abortion on a Friday.

On the Wednesday before, I called my mom and burst out crying. I told her I couldn't go through with the abortion. She responded, "I know you can't. Your father and I will still be down there Friday." I'd been against abortion all my life so she knew deep down inside I wanted to have my baby. Hearing her saying it was going to be okay gave me peace about my decision. My parent's support was very important to me. I immediately got off the phone and canceled the appointment. I realized that I tried to make a decision based off of what was best for everyone else but not what was best for me. God knew that I wouldn't be able to handle what came along with the decision to go through with an abortion. Instead, I was willing to go through whatever hardship that came along with being a young mother.

I called my son's father and told him I wasn't going through with the abortion. I was going to have my son whether he was in the picture or not. Of course, he was upset and his feelings towards not being ready remained the same. Thirteen years later, I have never called or cursed out my son's father for requiring me to raise my son on my own because I already knew there was a strong possibility he wouldn't be around. And he wasn't. There's no reason to get mad about something I already knew was going to happen and don't have any control over. Instead of getting angry, I did exactly what my father told me to do; I grew up quickly so that I could take care of my responsibility, my son.

Even though my son's dad wasn't an active father in his life, my son still had an active grandmother who made an effort to be in his life. I was truly thankful for that. She had no control over her son's decision to be absent but she made it very clear to me that she wanted to be in her grandson's life. Although she lived in NC, we would meet half way between our homes for her to get her grandson. Family is very important to me and I never kept my son from his dad's family. Being in that situation taught me a lot, especially to never judge anyone about their circumstances unless you have walked in that person's shoes. My family and friends were very supportive about my pregnancy. Being a young mother is never ideal but I knew I was going to be okay because my family was in my corner.

In 2006, I finished out my semester at Guilford College and came home in May. During that same time, my sister's condo was damaged when her neighbor's condo caught fire. So, she had to move back home as well. We were one happy family again all living under the same roof.

It was great being back home with my family. My mother and I really wanted a boy. She wanted to know how it would feel to have a boy that looked just like her because my brother didn't look anything

39

like her. Well, I did have a boy and he looked exactly like her. She absolutely loved being a grandmother and spoiled him rotten. Three months after I had my son, my mother became sick. And after three years of fighting her disease, she passed away. God knew that if I chose to abort my son, she would have never experienced being a grandmother. And I wouldn't have had the time to spend with her because I would have been away at school. I believe my son brought me home to my mother at exactly the right time. I don't believe it was a coincidence that my sister had to come home either.

When my mother passed away, it was a harsh reality that I wasn't able to accept. There were plenty of times when I no longer wanted to live; I wanted to give up. Then I remembered that I was still someone's mother and my son depended on me. In order to get through each day without her, I had to lie to myself, pretending my mom was on vacation. When she passed away, I still held my secret of sexual abuse and I could no longer share my pain since my Queen was gone.

Because I came from a loving home, I never looked for love, but I was still looking for something. Can you guess what that was? Protection! Because of my past trauma, I wanted to always feel safe as I grew older and started dating. In the back of my mind, I knew being sexually abused caused me to look at the world differently. I wanted a strong man as a partner, someone who would keep me safe. A street dude, with a street mentality and that's exactly how the father of my daughters carried himself. I knew no matter what, he would NEVER let anyone harm me or mistreat me. But even though he didn't let anyone else hurt me, that didn't stop him from hurting me himself. When I was with him, I felt protected from anyone and everybody while we were out but I still allowed him to hurt me. My only focus was on the fact that he wouldn't let anyone else hurt me.

Being unable to walk in my truth due to the unbearable pain caused me to make a lot of poor decisions. I knew the father of my daughters before my mom passed away. He was one of my clients; I braided his hair. When I first met him, I could immediately tell what kind of man he was. He was very attractive, so I assumed he went out with a lot of women. Even though he had a nine-to-five job, he still had a street mentality. He tried his hand and asked me to go out every time he came to have his hair done.

"What are you doing later?" he asked.

And I responded, "Going home to my son," every time. I didn't want any part of his game. He was really cool and we had great conversations but I knew we came from two different worlds.

As time went on, he remained persistent. He called me and told me to call him back but I only telephoned him when he wanted to make a hair appointment. I told him I wouldn't go out with him because I don't date my clients. I guess that was a valid excuse but it didn't stop him from trying. After a while, I got used to him asking me to go out and he got used to me saying no. During the next two years, he disappeared for long spans of time, then suddenly called me again out of nowhere. When I moved from the salon where I met him initially my old co-workers told him I had moved to a new location.

He gave me a call one day right after I lost my mom. He expressed that he also lost his grandmother around that same time. Months went by and I continued to braid his hair every so often. Then one day he called and he said he had a surprise for me. He came to my shop and all of his hair was cut off! He looked at me and said, "What's your excuse now? I'm no longer your client so can I take you out?" I kept my cool in front of him but deep down inside I thought, "Wow! This man is really serious." Yet, I still held my ground and remained professional with him. Remember, from the very beginning I knew he was someone that should stay in the friend zone, nothing more, nothing less.

Listen, Ladies, this man did not give up. Even though he didn't have hair for me to braid, every Friday he stopped by my shop to sit and just talk to my clients and me until we ran him off with a topic he didn't want to discuss. As time went on, he became like a friend that I knew liked me. I got comfortable around him, too comfortable. Then one day, he overheard me on the phone saying how I had nothing to do once I left work. The look on his face instantly said, "GOTCHA!" He asked me to ride to the Verizon store with him and I couldn't lie because he heard me say I was free for the rest of the day. Believe it or not, we had such a good time doing that errand, I ended up meeting him later that evening.

From that moment on, we were inseparable. It's crazy how he pursued me for two years but I always ran from him. I forgot all about the fact I knew we were from two different worlds. Our upbringing was different; he was from the city and I was from the suburbs. When you don't walk in your truth, you start to fill the void with activities and people that you already know are not right for you.

When my mom passed away, I stopped caring about the things that were once important to me. I stopped taking care of every-day tasks. I stopped paying my bills correctly and clearly forgot about all the lessons my mom taught me about taking care of your credit and paying bills on time. By the time I was 20, I had a credit score of 750 because my mother made sure we understood the importance of good credit. She could buy whatever she wanted because she had amazing credit. I messed my credit up because after losing the most important woman in my life, nothing else seemed to matter. My mother's passing was just too much to bear at times and being a responsible adult and paying my bills was just too much pressure.

Being sexually abused as a child also had a major impact on my life. I tried to go about life as if I was normal but I wasn't. I was deeply wounded and scarred but instead of dealing with the painful memories, I just acted like the incident never existed! Then one day I asked myself, "Jenise, why are you allowing this man to mistreat you as if you don't know how to be treated? You have a father who showed you how a man should treat you, love you, care for you, and respect you." None of his poor behavior towards me mattered because all I cared about was the fact that my ex wouldn't let anyone or anything hurt me!

Psychologically knowing that he was so overprotective of me gave me a sense of comfort. Being with him reassured me that another man would never be able to sexually abuse me again. His overprotection overshadowed the pain he caused me himself. It's like I was still that six-year-old little girl, wishing someone was there to protect me from the predator. I couldn't focus on the cheating, disrespectfulness, verbal abuse, or mistreatment because all I cared about was PROTECTION! My childhood trauma caused me to want the feeling of safety that I didn't have at that moment. But honestly, who could protect me from him?

This man chased me consistently for two years only to mistreat me once we got together and to this day, I still don't understand why. Maybe the chase was so exciting that once he 'won his prize,' he was no longer interested in making an effort. I spent five years with my ex, trying to change this man and help him see that I was a Good Woman. I wasn't the perfect woman but I can honestly say that my intentions in our relationship were always pure. The strain from our toxic relationship almost drove me to my death bed. One day, as we were arguing, I felt a shortness of breath and started hyperventilating. He thought I was being dramatic but when I was tested, my doctor diagnosed me with a heart condition.

I went to the doctor for a regular check-up. With each of my pregnancies, I had an EKG and it always came back normal. Well, after the argument, the test came back abnormal. Over the years of arguing and screaming at the top of my lungs, my heart was damaged. My doctor asked me if I was going to allow the person who argued with me to kill me. She mentioned to me she had the same heart condition but hers was more severe. When I asked her what she did to control her own heart condition, she said, "I stopped arguing!

Just like that, I realized that my kids needed me more than I needed to save and change this grown man! I said to myself, "Jenise, this man is going to be the death of you. Something has to change. It's not going to be him, so it needs to be you." Every time he did something to hurt me or I'd find out that he cheated, I always left. The problem was never me being strong enough to leave; instead, my problem was being strong enough not to take him back. He always reeled me back in with all his broken promises that he never kept. He always told me he would do better, and he would change, but the change only lasted for a short period after I took him back. I wanted to believe what he told me and I kept praying one day he would be true to his words. But his actions never changed. I often had those moments when I had a sudden epiphany that I needed to walk away from this relationship. But of course, leaving is easier said than done.

Even after I was diagnosed with a heart condition, I still didn't leave. I just made a mental note about having a heart condition and how the doctor told me I could die from it if I continued to argue. Being sexually abused as a child made me want to help everyone, save everyone, be nice to everyone. I never wanted to cause anyone pain; I always wanted to help someone through their pain. If I could prevent anyone from feeling the pain I experienced; I did all that I could to help them. I offered help to others that I should have been offering myself. The thought of hurting anyone intentionally only made me think about the hurt that my offender caused me.

My past trauma made me desire protection in a man instead of looking for a Godly man. This problem was too BIG for me to handle on my own, but it was NEVER too big for God. I gave my burden to God and I allowed for him to carry it. I prayed for strength to be able to face the fear of accepting I was a victim of sexual abuse. Once I was able to talk about being molested without guilt or shame, I was able to identify what my problem really was. The problem wasn't my ex for mistreating me; the problem was me and that I ALLOWED my ex to mistreat me! By reading my Bible more and truly trusting Him, I've learned that GOD was all the protection I needed. I didn't have to be mistreated to feel protected. With God, I felt loved and protected. I just wish I made a decision to walk in this truth a lot sooner.

So, Ladies, I know it's going to hurt to open up about situations you've tried to forget but I promise you, give that burden to God. Pray that He sets you free from that load and truly gives you the understanding that we aren't meant to carry any burdens. He won't fail you so for once in your life, you will feel whole again!

I make it very clear to my coaching clients that the process of healing can be painful but continuing to avoid and ignore those scars will only hurt you more. I am finally free now that I made the choice to walk in my truth. I was a prisoner in my own mind; my childhood trauma kept me captive for so long. It feels liberating to know that even though my past trauma caused me so much pain, that same trauma led me to fulfill my purpose. The truth hurts but the truth also sets you free.

Ask yourself, "What is the Real Problem?" What makes you feel like others should be allowed to treat you as far less than you deserve? What causes you to feel like you aren't worthy enough and think you should stay with someone who doesn't recognize your worth? What makes you feel as though your world can't go on without him? You are struggling with a deeper issue and it's time to deal with the underlying problems. It's time to stop allowing that issue or emotion to control your life. The truth hurts but I also know that the truth will set you free.

If you never learn how to depart from your Past, you'll never know what it's like to Arrive.

Once you realize that your shortcomings in life don't depreciate your value or your worth as a woman; you'll understand that how you choose to treat yourself is now the Standard of how you'll allow others to treat you.

Ladies, **Accept** your truth, **Heal** from your truth, **Own** it knowing it's your truth, and then **Walk** in your truth with your head held high!

His Truth

We must understand not all men are given the tools to properly love you to your standards; his standard may be all that he knows.

— Jenise McNair

Most of the time we are so quick to blame all of our problems on the men who mistreat us because, of course, they are the ones who conduct themselves in a manner that makes us feel disrespected. After being in a dysfunctional relationship for five years, I learned that the issue goes much deeper than we think. Much deeper than his actions and much deeper than his choices. In the previous chapter, I wrote about "Her truth." So, what is the honest reason for you to be with a man that mistreats you?

Well, believe it or not, most men who behave in an abusive manner, whether physical, mental or emotional, are dealing with their own deep-seeded issues that cause them to conduct themselves in that manner. They battle with deep-rooted issues that only come to the surface when they are angry or unable to process an emotion. They might have been molested, verbally or physically abused, abandoned, or just raised in a very dysfunctional household for their entire lives. Most of the time the anger that comes from a man has nothing to do with you, but it has everything to do with how he feels about himself on the inside.

The first woman that a little boy falls in love with is most likely his mother, and the first man that a little boy admires and looks up to is his father. A father is supposed to give his son a part of his identity, to help mold him and guide him into becoming his own man. A mother nurtures her son and is always there with her shoulder to lean on when things get tough. A mother's love is unconditional; it's something that no child should have to live without.

Can you imagine a little boy growing up without a mother's love or without a father's support and guidance to mold him into the man he one day will be? Imagine never having a mother to kiss and hug him or a father to look at him proudly and say, "Well done, Son." Unfortunately, there are a lot of boys and men who never had caring parents. They had to grow up on their own, trying to overcome and understand why their parents were not a part of their lives. They navigate through life, trying to raise themselves with little or no guidance. I've met quite a few men who've told me they had to grow up on their own due to various circumstances, including abandonment, single mothers who had to work late, or the loss of their parents at a young age.

A little boy's relationship with his mother and father usually plays a major role in his identity as he grows up. I believe a man's childhood and his upbringing has a lot to do with his perception of life. If his mother mistreated him, did not care for him, or always let him down, that may affect his perception of women in general, once he becomes a man. What makes him trust that any woman could love him or be there for him, if his own mother who birthed him couldn't? I realize not all men who had to live through not having a mother or father around have issues with anger or trust, but there's more than a few who do struggle with these concerns. After experiencing a bad relationship, when women go on dates, one of the first questions we often ask is, "How is your relationship with your mother?" We want to know because most women believe how a man treats his mother has a lot to do with how he will love, respect, and honor them.

A father who shares the same body parts as his son, clearly understands the makeup of a little boy because a father was once a little boy himself. He knows what it is like for a boy to go through puberty and to understand his hormones. Without a father in his life, that same little boy is left to speak to his mother about those uncomfortable topics. I can't imagine how that embarrassment possibly makes that little boy feel inside. Probably angry! Probably frustrated! Probably confused! At the end of the day, he sees that other kids have fathers to answer these questions but he has to figure out these hormonal changes and how to navigate life on his own.

How does a mother look at her child and try to give a valid reason why his father isn't around, other than telling him the honest truth? Even if his father is in jail, how do you explain why he chose crime over staying with his son? There's no winning solution in this situation. And as a single mother, all you can do is pray for your son. For little boys who grow up without either parent, what are they to do? Let society and the streets raise them?

I believe most guys who are or were in the streets are there because no one was at home to guide them or keep them on a straight and narrow path. There wasn't any structure or discipline given to them. Other boys turn to the streets because they have too much time on their hands. They may have parents in their household, but they don't participate in any extracurricular activities so they go outside and hang in the streets daily. Sometimes the streets become their family; the streets seem more loyal, family-oriented, and trustworthy than their very own family at home. The streets teach them how to survive and give them some form of security to know there are others who are going through similar issues. There's a certain bond that takes place when they are in the streets, mentored by someone who was once in their situation but now has a better life. Younger boys enjoy having a hero, a role model, or their own father to look up to. Unfortunately, some boys must do the best they can with what they have.

I also believe these boys grow up with invisible pain, looking for other outlets in life to fill the void in their hearts. They may question why they had to go through certain struggles or losses that other kids didn't experience. Hurt boys grow into hurt men and we have to understand that the childhood anger didn't go anywhere, the frustration didn't go anywhere. He just learned how to suppress those emotions. When this same little boy grows up into a man, he'll meet a woman, and Bam! When life starts to get the best of them, all the unresolved problems and unanswered questions start to overtake him emotionally. Those stressors may cause him to take all his frustrations out on the woman and the relationship. A man who is not happy within will never be able to see a woman's worth. At the end of the day, he can't even recognize his own worth.

Ladies, we must understand not all men are given the tools to properly love you to your standards. His standard of love may be all that he knows how to give or all he's received himself. We have to stop dealing with men who have untreated wounds from their childhood and their past. In order for a relationship to be healthy, both woman and man need to come together, already whole. Both individuals must take the time to learn about themselves, understanding who they are and what they want out of life. They must embrace who they were, who they are, and everything they hope to become. They must deal with any past trauma and pain that interferes with their self-happiness and peace. Both people must take accountability for their own happiness and not go into a relationship expecting the other person to be the ultimate reason for their happiness. A man and woman who are whole know who they are and what they want. Anything that falls beneath those standards isn't acceptable.

Having a mother or father who abandons you would make anyone question their worth. But again, we don't pay attention to signs and red flags. Those signs include when a man says, "I don't deserve you," or "Why would you want to be with a man like me?" When men say things like that, it is because they perceive that they are unworthy of something good. If they go their whole life always experiencing negative circumstances, it is hard for them to accept when good circumstances present themselves. Some men already formed patterns of always expecting the worst. They believe if anything positive happens to them, it's too good to be true so they try to sabotage it. It's the "I'm going to hurt you before you hurt me" type of mentality. Their perception of life is based on their own personal experience which is something we have no power to change.

Oftentimes women are destined for hurt from the beginning, but when you love someone, it's hard to accept the truth! Once we are in love, we never want to accept that walking away from the relationship is the best decision to make. We never want to focus on their actions but instead we only want to focus on the potential we saw in the man we chose to love. We don't want to accept that we didn't choose the right man. We don't want to accept that we can't love a man past his pain. We don't want to accept that we can't fix him. We don't want to accept that he may not want to get married. Women are so quick to try and alter the reality of a relationship and make adjustments instead of accepting and understanding the truth cannot be altered.

One of our main mistakes when dating is that we don't take the time to really know these men we commit to. It is very important for us to take the time to get to know a man that we are interested in. We have to use discernment and wisdom to discover if this man fits in our world and lives up to our standards. Time truly tells all. If we learn to focus on what we want most instead of what we want at the moment, we could save ourselves from unnecessary pain.

In my opinion, most men who are abusive deal with a lot of anger inside. They are hurting and they choose to deal with their pain in a very unhealthy way for both them and the people they hurt with their actions. Many men who are abusive either saw or experienced abuse growing up and became a product of their environment. Everyone deals and copes with pain in different ways. Some men use sleeping with a bunch of women as a way to fill a void. They could be trying to fill the void of love, attention, or affection they never received while growing up. They are searching for a cure for their pain but no matter how many women they sleep with, that void will remain until they confront their issues.

How many of us have dealt with a man who just wouldn't be faithful, no matter how many times he got caught or he said he will never cheat again, yet it still happened? We try to justify this behavior and the pain that they cause when we should really take those actions at face value and learn to walk away. We choose to stay because ultimately, we just want the man that we love to act right and treat us the way we should be treated. We don't want to accept that maybe they aren't capable of loving us or treating us right. Some men really operate in fear; fearful of allowing someone in, only for them to be hurt again. They harbor their childhood traumas and truly believe no one is capable of loving them. How can a man who's broken, honestly believe a woman is capable of loving him unconditionally when he feels like his own mother didn't?

I don't think we truly take the time to understand men. A jealous and overly-possessive man is an insecure man. When a man isn't secure within himself because of his own personal insecurities that developed as a child, there are pieces to his emotional puzzle that are missing. If he's not comfortable with who he is, then being in control of a situation or relationship is the only way to ease his mind. Feeling like he is in control allows him to deal with circumstances he can't change. That power lets him do things his way to reassure his comfort. Ladies, it's so important to get to know a guy and his background because his history plays a major part of who he is.

Do you ever wonder why no matter what you do or say, you can never please him? No matter how hard you try to show him how much you love him, it seems like your efforts are never enough. Truthfully, no matter what you do, it will never be enough until he deals with himself and his issues that he pretends doesn't exist. He can't conquer what he doesn't confront. As long as he acts like nothing is wrong, he will continue to take his anger or frustration out on you because you're the closest one to him. It's easier to take his frustration out on you because he knows how much you love him; he knows that it isn't easy to make the decision to leave him. He takes advantage of your love for him and uses you as an outlet for his frustration and pain. You're guilty by association when he isn't strong enough to deal with his problems in a healthy way.

It's so important for you to realize that the best action you can take is to walk away from a man that isn't ready to love you. He doesn't even know how to love himself. A man has to want to change in order to change. If he doesn't think anything is wrong with him or his behavior, then change will never happen. If he tells you that he's going to change and you only see those results for a short amount of time, it's clear he only made those adjustments to win you back. A woman can influence a man to want to do better but ultimately he has to be the one to take action and live up to his full potential.

In my healing process, I had to understand that some people only know what they learned as they grew up. If they knew better, maybe they would do better. This understanding helped me with my healing by being able to show compassion to those people who only knew what they were shown. I had to understand everyone isn't fortunate enough to grow up in a loving environment. What may be easy for me, might be harder for someone else. Some men can only work with the tools that they were given. I'm not taking up for these men; wrong is wrong and they mistreated you. But I am saying that they may believe that the way they treat you is a form of love. Their mothers may have loved them but cursed them out as children and now they think it's okay to curse you out. Cursing is just another form of communication to them. But you may not have been raised in that manner so to you, cursing may be flat-out disrespectfulness.

Ladies, there are some things you just can't help a man get through, unless he really wants your help and is willing to help himself first. One thing that I have learned about men, is that many of them don't know how to deal with their emotions very well. They are human too and they do get emotional, just like women. The problem is men have trouble dealing with their emotions because most of the time they don't want to deal with something they have no control over. So that's how the problem begins; they take all of the feelings and emotions about their issues and they tuck them away as if they never existed. They don't understand that those emotions are only going to resurface later but in a different form that isn't healthy for the men or anyone who's close to them. A man has to learn how to walk in his truth as well.

I thought if my title changed, the behavior of my daughter's father was going to change as well, but it didn't. I left him over and over again but he always found a way to reel me back in. He proposed to me at a time that we weren't even together. I said yes! The same person who called me bitches and hoes every chance he got; was the same person who looked me in my eyes and asked me to be his wife. As his fiancée, I thought his behavior towards me would be different. From his girlfriend, to the mother of his child, and then to his fiancée, I had to make a very tough decision. Did I want to become his wife thinking once I said, "I do," his poor behavior towards me would change? I grew up in a two-parent household and my parents were married for thirty years before my mom passed. I knew how much I valued marriage and getting married to only get a divorce later wasn't an option for me. I couldn't say, "I do," just so he could make an honest woman out of me. Instead, I had to be honest with myself and accept change wouldn't take place just because I became his wife.

Being a woman and raising my son is one of the hardest endeavors I ever had to do and it is still a work in progress. One year ago, I got one of the most-feared phone calls a mother could ever receive. The Dean at my son's school called to tell me that a girl claimed my son allegedly sexually assaulted her. My heart instantly stopped beating as I tried to process what she said. I left work and made my way to his school.

My son and I have a very open relationship and we often talk about life and how the world is set up. So, I asked him what happened. He told me he was with the girl after school and they were fooling around. Apparently, another student saw them and told many other students the next day. The girl later went to the office crying and told the Dean my son assaulted her. The Dean stated to us, if my son didn't admit to assaulting the girl, her parents were going to press charges against him.

I looked my son in the eyes and asked him to tell me the truth. He told me he didn't assault her; that fooling around was consensual and she never told him to stop! No sexual intercourse was involved, just touching and feeling. I told the Dean that I believed my son and I wasn't going to allow him to admit to something he didn't do. We would see the girl in court, if that's what we had to do. Later that evening, the girl's story changed. She admitted that he didn't sexually assault her.

So many men are behind bars because women lied to get out of trouble or just tried to get back at them and intentionally ruined their lives. Once again, I talked to my son and warned him about putting himself in compromising situations when it comes to girls. These are the moments as a single mother when you wish a Father was present. It can be very difficult and challenging as a mother to play both roles.

When my son was younger, I didn't have to answer many questions regarding why his father wasn't around consistently. I used to say phrases like, "Oh, he has to work," or "You will see him soon." But as he started to get older, there wasn't much I could do to cover for his father because he knew it wasn't the truth. As years passed, he saw his father on holidays or spring break. He often told me, "Yeah, my dad said he was going to drive up next weekend." But I knew his dad never would, based on his track record.

I used to ask, "Does it bother you that your father tells you that he's going to come up but he never does?"

And his response was always, "Nope! I don't care."

As a mother, I knew deep-down inside that he did care. But because he couldn't control the situation and make his father come see him, it was easier for him to suppress his feelings and emotions by simply telling himself that it didn't matter. As a woman and as a mother, I had to ask myself, "What can I do to help my son cope with the fact that his father doesn't make an effort to be in his life consistently?" I knew that society often labeled little boys and men based on whether or not their fathers were in their lives. I didn't want that judgment to be an excuse for my son. I didn't want this issue to hold him back from becoming the man God called him to be. I desired for him to get whatever he wanted out of life.

Between the ages of eight to almost eleven years old, my son began to have behavioral issues. He wouldn't do what he was supposed to do in school, talked back to me when I asked him to do something, or acted completely rebellious. Despite the help from his godfather and my brother, who play vital roles in his life, he still continued to act out. They tried to hold him accountable and give him structure. My son tried to leverage the reality that his godfather couldn't always get to him because he lives in North Carolina. But when they finally saw each other, you can believe my son was in for it. My older cousin Mel told me to search online for a therapist but I was so against him seeing one. I just didn't want my son to be labeled as anything other than what God called him to be. But I had to trust God and believe that counseling might be the best thing for him.

The therapist I found for my son was absolutely the best. As a mother, I needed to do whatever was necessary for my son to be able to express and deal with his emotions in a healthy way. I didn't want him to bottle up any emotions about how his dad wasn't involved or allow his anger to turn into something that was against his best interest. It's crazy how a complete stranger could give advice that clicked but when his godfather, his uncle, or I gave similar advice it went right over his head.

After two months of therapy, I started seeing a tremendous change in my son. When I asked him to do something or when he got reprimanded, the way he responded completely changed. I honestly couldn't believe it. Before he started therapy, he had a serious attitude and anger problem. I felt like the root of his anger came from the misunderstanding of why his father didn't make an effort to be around. I wanted my son to deal with the inconsistency of his father in a healthy way. We've learned how to get through the issue without him using it as an excuse to fail later in life. I now teach my son to not focus on the circumstances he can't change but to be thankful for my brother and his godfather for choosing to step up and be there for him during these impressionable times. As my son gets older, he recognizes that he has an army of people who love him and support him.

I brought up that situation with my son only to show that many men out in the world today have deep-rooted issues from childhood that they never took the time to honestly deal with. How many men have tried to tuck away their feelings and emotions when they were young only to have them resurface as they got older? But at that point, those issues resurfaced and caused them to deal with their emotions in a violent or abusive way.

It is so important for men to be able to deal with their emotions and they need to start learning how to do this at a young age. Women are able to handle their emotions better than men because anytime we feel emotional, the first thing that we do is cry and let our feelings out. Most little boys, however, are taught not to cry, even at a very young age. At the first sign of tears, we often say, "What are you crying for? You better stop all that crying and man up!" Why do we tell little boys to 'man up' when clearly, they are little boys? They are human; boys have feelings and emotions too! But we've trained our little boys who become grown men to suppress and hold in their emotions. It's not healthy for them to bottle up these feelings that truly causes many problems in adulthood.

I get it, we want our little boys to be tough, we want them to grow up and be strong. But how can we raise young boys to become men without causing them to make poor decisions because they can't channel how they feel inside? How can we convey to our young boys that it's okay to cry and release their emotions without reinforcing that it's okay to cry when life doesn't go their way? How do we show our young boys it's very important to learn how to deal with their feelings and emotions without feeling ashamed? That they can truly express how they feel without seeming soft or weak in the process? Do you know there are millions and millions of men every day who truly don't know how to handle or express their emotions in a *healthy* way? Women are left to figure out why all these men have so much difficulty trying to effectively communicate how they feel or show some type of emotions.

We brainwash our young boys into thinking that crying, showing emotions, or expressing how they feel is only something that women should do. Then when a man starts crying or showing any type of emotion, the first thing we say is, "Oh, he is soft," or "He's weak. Just throw the whole man in the trash!!!" How we view men who show emotion is terrible! Why is it that men must choose between our version of manliness and emotional healthiness?

Men and women are wired differently in a lot of ways, but there are a few major areas that are made the exact same way, including our hearts, which give us the ability to love and feel, and our sensory nerves, which cause us to feel pain. Men weren't created to have babies and they couldn't even if they tried. They don't naturally have what is needed to give birth, which clearly shows that childbirth wasn't something they were supposed to ever be able to do. But if a man wasn't created to cry, then he wouldn't have the tear ducts to allow him to do so. Our hearts and our sensory nerves operate in the same manner when it comes to men and women. It's normal to have reactions toward the pain and the emotions we feel. A man who can't process how he feels is a man that will eventually explode with frustration from built-up emotions. Most of the time, the explosion isn't going to result in something positive either.

When you think about the expectations placed on men, their lack of emotion is why men really aren't good communicators at all and women usually are very good communicators. We are good communicators because we are encouraged to speak about how we feel and talk about our emotions, even at a very young age. If I happen to say something to my oldest daughter that doesn't make her feel good, she will definitely go out of her way to let me know. And she makes sure I have a full understanding not to say those words again because they hurt her feelings. It's a part of our normal function as women to communicate our feelings but it's not considered normal for males to express their feelings.

This unfortunate double standard means that a man who shows his feelings is often considered a weakling. Grown women are allowed to pout, act spoiled, or even cry when they don't get their way because that's what we learned as little girls and it was considered acceptable. That same standard wasn't the case for boys; they were taught to suppress any emotions they felt and they continue to compress their emotions as grown men. At some point, we have to break this negative cycle. We cannot diminish our value as women because we want to help heal and love a man past his pain. Walking in our truth as men and women will allow us to accept the things we cannot change about our past and make the effort to change the things about ourselves that we still can. Our painful truth doesn't define us nor does it have to keep us from having all of our hearts' desires, but we must learn how to deal with our pain in a healthy way.

Ladies, I just want you to understand that if you are broken and he is broken, the two of you will never be whole until you part ways and deal with your own issues at hand. Work on yourself and figure out who you are and what you want. You can't save him; all you can do is save yourself and leave everything else to God. Especially with teen-age and young-adult relationships, we have to allow young men to grow up and figure out what they want. They shouldn't be trying to heal all of their issues while in the midst of a relationship. As we already know, there are grown men who still don't know what they want and that's okay, as long as they aren't wasting your time while trying to figure it out.

As women, when dating it's important to understand, we can't fix anyone but ourselves and we can't raise grown men either. Each man is the only person who knows his truth and can make the decision to walk in it. We don't have control over anyone but ourselves. If a man doesn't treat you the way that you deserve, you have to be content with walking away, no matter how many years you already invested and no matter what people say. We have to learn how to accept the truth, be wise about the situation, and truly learn how to do what's best for us. Even if that means walking away from the man you love.

Remember, we can't raise grown men, so let's just stop trying! It's already hard enough to change ourselves, so our main priority in a relationship shouldn't be to change our man. If you find yourself entering a relationship with a man you want to change, walk away! You should have never started that relationship in the first place. The truth will set everyone free and men have to walk in their truth as well. Entering a relationship or staying in one just to fill your own voids isn't worth the pain that will come along with that relationship. Always choose to do what's best for you and don't ever apologize for it!

Remember, how you choose to treat yourself, will always be the Standard of how you'll allow others to treat you.

Silent Abuse

And when he tells you, you ain't nothin', don't believe him;
and if he can't learn to love you, you should leave him.
'Cuz sista you don't need him.

— Tupac Shakur

Can you imagine how many women across the world suffer
from some type of abuse in silence, all alone? By contrast,
the U.S. Department of Justice finds that women make up
84% of spouse abuse victims. Whether physical, mental, or
emotional abuse, many women encounter one of these
types of abuse but remain silent. Why? Because in our
society, women find every reason to tear down the next
woman instead of lifting her up. We are so quick to pass
judgment about another woman's situation, that we never
really take the time to try to understand or help the woman
who's in need. As women, we could be so much more
powerful if we learned how to stand together and empower
one another; to build off each other's strengths and truly
encourage one another to rise above.

It's a dreadful place when you feel like you are all alone in
your situation and there's no way out. You don't want to
speak about your problems to anyone because you're afraid
they might judge you instead of listening or helping. You
force yourself to suppress the feelings of pain you are going
through when you are around your friends and family.
What you may not realize is that a lot of women are going
through very similar circumstances.

How often do we choose to mask the pain that seems so unbearable, only to become numb to those hurts over time?

Less than a century ago, abusive relationships were even more prevalent, and sometimes were even expected. Whether emotional abuse or even physical abuse, your relatives may have suffered at the hands of their husbands. Times were different than they are now; women did not hold high-paying jobs and few were able to really be independent or take care of themselves and their children all alone. Men were the sole financial providers. Because women often felt like there was nowhere to go, they were more likely to accept abuse from their husbands. They often knew about their husband's mistresses but felt like they had to accept their lot in life. They had a family to take care of, so they endured endless and untold pain.

After my twenty-first birthday, my father shared with me about his childhood. He expressed that he grew up in a very dysfunctional home, filled with domestic violence. My grandmother was a victim of abuse in her marriage. My father told me stories of how he watched my grandfather beat on my grandmother. There's an older movie called, *What's Love Got to Do with It* that tells Tina Turner's life story of how she was abused. My dad mentioned to me my grandmother was beat on by her husband just as bad, if not worse. The violence and abuse became my uncle's and my dad's normality as children. My father mentioned that my grandmother suffered from broken ribs, black eyes, busted lips, and frequent trips to the hospital due to the abuse. There were times after she was beaten that my grandmother was unrecognizable. Domestic violence in their house and in society as a whole during that time was accepted.

My father also expressed to me that my grandfather had multiple mistresses and didn't come home for days at a time, while his car was parked down the street, right outside his mistress' house. He didn't even try to hide the fact that he had affairs with other women. He said his father was a cool man, so much that all the guys wanted to be like him and all the women wanted to be with him. I used to ask my dad, "Why didn't Grandma leave? What made her feel like she had to stay? Grandma had her own money." He responded, " we sometimes left and went to her parents house but always ended up coming back home. Then, the situation continued as before, that "vicious cycle."

At that moment, it was so easy to ask my father, "Why wouldn't she just leave him?" Yet, I also ended up subjecting myself to all forms of abuse while I struggled with the decision to leave my violent relationship. Generational curses are real and I allowed myself to make the same choices my grandmother did and I wasn't even married. Yet, I still felt like I had no way out.

My father continued to tell me how one day, when he was 12 and my uncle was 14, they jumped on his father because he was beating his mother. They went flying across the room because they tried to protect my grandmother. But my grandfather knew as they got older, he was going to have to answer to them every time he took out his anger on his wife. They weren't going to stay little long.

Even when my father was in high school, the vicious cycle of abuse continued and nothing changed. Until, one day while my grandfather was asleep, my grandmother took a big, glass, gallon jug and broke it on his face. When my father looked up, all he saw was my grandmother running out of the house with one shoe on, while my grandfather screamed and cursed as blood gushed down his face. My father rushed into the room to see if his dad was okay but he just cursed and said "that bitch hit me upside my head." My granddad had to get numerous stitches and had a black eye for about a year. My dad expressed to me that he loved my granddad because he was an awesome father even though he was a horrible husband. But my granddad didn't understand how his poor behavior as a husband still damaged his children. Watching their mother get beat up affected their ability to focus in school because all they could think about was the violence that took place at home. My grandfather also had a mistress which disturbed his family's balance as well.

It took a long time for my dad to tell me the truth about what really happened to my grandfather. Growing up with domestic violence in your home can have a major impact on the lives of your children. Seeing your mother get cursed out and beat up for your whole entire childhood can really cause some damage. And although the abuse affected my father, it definitely damaged my uncle.

One day, when my father was home from college, my grandmother and grandfather had some people over to their house. My grandfather and my dad were sitting on the side porch talking, when they saw my uncle walk up. My dad noticed that he had a magazine in his hand. The next thing you know, my uncle dropped the magazine and my dad realized he was holding a gun. My father turned to his dad to tell him about the gun but my uncle shot my dad in the back first. Then he shot my grandfather in the chest. After my dad realized he was shot, he looked at my granddad and saw that he was wounded and coughing up blood. My father ran inside to check on my grandmother who had also been shot in the stomach by my uncle. My dad realized that my granddad's best friend was shot in the chest as well. My granddad and his best friend were pronounced dead on the scene. My grandmother was shot in her stomach but the bullet hit her rib and ricocheted through her arm. As a result, the nerves in her arm were damaged and she never regained feeling in two of her fingers. The bullet that hit my dad missed his spine by a fraction of an inch. He could have been paralyzed or even lost his life!

My uncle stole a car to flee the scene, then hijacked a plane at gunpoint at a small airport at Woodbridge, Virginia. The pilot told him that he needed to make an emergency landing and landed on a highway in Fayetteville, North Carolina. My uncle left the plane and hijacked another car at gunpoint so he could head to another airport. That airport in Fayetteville was where the FBI agents apprehended him.

No one knows what triggered my uncle to do such madness but my grandmother felt like her abuse over the years played a major part psychologically. My grandmother got the best lawyer for him so he wouldn't do jail time considering all the accounts charged against him. Knowing the history of the family and the abuse they all suffered over the years, as a mother she felt responsible for my uncle's actions. My uncle never did any jail time but he did have to go to a mental institution for 20 years. Once those 20 years were up, he was released under a conditional release which stated that he had to be supervised and evaluated. He ended up living with my grandmother again.

My dad said the story was all over the news but once he got out of the hospital, he decided to return to college two weeks after his release. My father mentioned that this situation could have broken him if he allowed it to. He persevered through the pain and vowed to himself that he wouldn't become a product of his environment. Not only did he lose his father but he also lost his brother as well. My dad and grandmother later found out from a cousin that my uncle borrowed money from his dad which he used to purchase the gun. He showed one of his cousins that he bought a gun, but the cousin didn't realize what he planned to use it for.

My uncle was never the same after he got out of the mental institution. He became very paranoid, because of what he did, and he always felt people were after him. My grandmother passed away and my dad became my uncle's guardian. Of course, because of what he did, he still had to be supervised to a certain extent and go to the hospital for periodic evaluations. If it wasn't for my dad telling me what happened, I would've never known his tragic story because my dad always showed compassion, grace, love, and support toward my uncle.

My dad is such an amazing man. He lost his dad, brother, mother, and wife yet he continues to make an effort to become the best man and father he could possibly be, despite all the pain he's had to endure. I was completely shocked after hearing about his childhood. To know he experienced such trauma and was still able to look at life in such a positive way, made me change my perspective towards life. My father had a lot of reasons to make him want to give up but he didn't. I appreciate my father for being honest about his childhood. Sometimes parents think keeping family secrets is what's best but in all honesty, keeping secrets does more damage in the long run; especially if it deceives you to believe something that isn't true. Because I knew this situation took place and understood how much abuse and domestic violence affected my father and uncle, I never thought I would allow anyone to abuse me in any way.

My granddad never knew his father growing up, and his mother had him at a young age. One day, she dropped him at his grandmother's house but never came back to get him. So, he was raised by his grandmother. I'm sure my grandfather felt that he had been abandoned by both parents. He was a very smart man, and attended Howard University after serving in the army for two years. He made All-CIAA in football and swimming and was a member of the Omega Si Phi Fraternity while in college. After graduating, he obtained his masters degree from Massachusetts in 1952, at the age of 25. He also was able to speak fluent French. My grandfather was the head football coach for Spingarn High School in Washington, DC for more than ten years. He was well known, highly respected and very successful.

But no matter how successful he was, the past trauma and pain from his childhood caused my granddad to behave with violence and infidelity. He chose to use these unhealthy acts in order to cope. *The height of a person's success means nothing, if their self-worth is measured so low.* Unfortunately, success doesn't bring someone true inner happiness.

How you gonna win when you ain't right within

— Lauryn Hill

Knowing my dad's story definitely played a major role in my decision to leave the toxic relationship I was in because I realized if I didn't leave, my children would be affected. Especially knowing how a lifetime of abuse, damaged my dad and most definitely my uncle. Even though my father grew up in a very abusive environment, he made it his business not to become a product of his environment. He never called my mother out by her name or even cursed at her and he never put his hands on her in anger. As I grew up, my dad always spoke to me with respect and treated me like a princess. Even when he was disappointed in me, his calm respect never changed. Unfortunately, there are some women who experienced being called out their name, even by their own father.

I understand that fear causes us to be hesitant when making decisions and we're so scared of change and so afraid of the unknown. Fear causes us to stay in relationships we shouldn't be in and prevents us from thinking a better situation is possible. I see how and why most women in the past stayed in abusive and unhealthy marriages. But I can't understand why women today still feel like we are stuck and we can't leave our abusive and unhealthy relationships.

The reason I didn't want to leave my toxic relationship was because I was in love, like most of us. I hoped and believed that he would change. I hoped he would one day tap into the potential I saw inside of him. I wanted to believe that his behavior towards me would one day change. I thought by enduring the endless pain caused by him, I would show him how much I loved him and how I wasn't willing to give up on him so easily. He was also the father of my two young daughters and I didn't think I could afford childcare since they were so young at the time. Outside of really loving him and not wanting to give up on him, there were times when we "broke up" and he gave me a hard time about providing money for our daughters. He was never consistent about giving me money to support our girls when we weren't together. Anytime I called him about money for our daughters, he said something degrading and made it seem like I was harassing him.

I was over the physical part of our relationship because of how many times he'd cheated. So, when I took him back, it wasn't even about the sex. I really just prayed and wanted him to change for the better. There were times when he wouldn't cooperate and he made my life harder because I was left to figure it out. Once I was pregnant with my youngest daughter, I decided to stay home with the girls because I couldn't afford childcare, let alone a mortgage, utilities, or car expenses. At the time, my father was still trying to get accustomed to being alone after losing my mother and covering his own expenses with just his retirement check, so I really felt stuck. We broke up and got back together so many times I stopped counting. My youngest daughter was conceived and we weren't even together at the time.

My oldest daughter got sick one day with a fever of 104°. He met me at the hospital as we were both concerned. In the previous months, we were not together nor did we even communicate. When they released my daughter from the hospital, he said he would stop by and check on her. He stopped by the next day while she was asleep. But instead of leaving, he stayed; the next thing you know, we were having sex. Two weeks later I took a pregnancy test and I was pregnant. The vicious cycle continued, but now with two children involved.

Abuse comes in so many forms and a lot of women don't even realize they are being abused. If you don't like the way a man talks to you, that is a form of abuse. If he always points out what's wrong with you or belittles you, that is a form of abuse. If he is the sole financial provider but makes you beg for money, that is also a form of abuse. Abuse isn't always when a man puts his hands on you. Abuse is when someone beats you down, whether its form is physical, verbal, emotional, or mental.

Manipulation was something my daughters' father tried to use to avoid holding himself accountable when he was wrong. He often accused me of cheating because of his own guilty conscience. He felt that I smiled too much whenever I was in another man's presence, which meant to him, I was interested in that man. Standing up for what I believed always meant I was going against him or taking someone else's side. He considered my kind and bubbly personality as a disrespectful attribute to him whenever we were in public. Being with him meant I had to choose to have no voice, alter who I was as a person, and stroke his ego all so that he could feel secure as a man.

There were times my daughters' father tried to hurt me. He called me all types of names and claimed that our daughters weren't his. He never wanted to take a paternity test which was just another way to get under my skin, belittle me, and try to control the narrative. I even told him, if he thought our daughters weren't his, then he could go down to the courthouse and sign his rights over. He later mentioned that he tried but the court told him he couldn't because he signed the affidavit and birth certificate. It's very hurtful for a man to deny his children, especially when you know he's the father. I allowed him to hurt me but I wasn't going to allow him to harm my daughters. Once he denied them, I blocked him for almost three months. Looking back, I was wrong for stooping down to his level and giving him the reaction he was seeking. But my motherly instincts made me want to protect my daughters during that time.

Some men deny their children out of anger, which is a form of emotional abuse. Being abused crushes your spirit and takes away your self-worth. Some women know when they are being abused but they justify it by making excuses for their abusers. I know I did! I always made excuses for him, whether I blamed it on alcohol or the pain and anger he refused to deal with. How people choose to treat you is just a reflection of how they feel about themselves. You can't expect a man to see the good in you as a woman if he can't even see the good in himself as a man.

Love is powerful, especially when you choose to love someone more than you love yourself. Your happiness is never a priority. Again, we make excuses before we accept that abuse is taking place. The question remains, why do we take this kind of abuse when we don't have to? Growing up in a household with two loving parents, I honestly couldn't understand why I allowed myself to go through an abusive relationship.

How many times will you allow a man to disrespect you by calling you out by name? How many times will you allow a man to disrespect you by coming home at all hours, in the middle of the night? To continuously cheat on you and have another woman in his life? Of course, when they get caught, they instantly become apologetic and we forgive them like everything is normal. No, they aren't sorry; they are just sorry they got caught. Most men will continue doing whatever they are doing until they get caught. Cheating is definitely a form of emotional abuse because it breaks your spirit and makes you think you aren't good enough. Why do men apologize to get you back but then cheat on you again? Because they take our love for granted!

I was young when my relationship started and had never been exposed to the type of behavior that my ex demonstrated to me. A lot of stuff I experienced with him, I'd only seen on TV or heard about it around me, mostly from older women. I honestly never thought in a million years that I would remain stuck for as long as I did, going through the misery he put me through. But that word "love" can cause you to take the wrong turn down "Do Not Drive Boulevard." It's the potential in a man that causes us to make that turn, believing and loving someone more than we believe in and love ourselves. What happens when you make a turn down a street that you weren't supposed to make? You get lost and confused trying to find your way out. My point is, we make decisions that we have no business making.

I never had a hard time leaving; the problem was I believed him when he said he would change and I kept taking him back. I was so gung-ho about his potential and his words that I didn't allow his actions to speak to me. As women, we often mistake love and what it stands for. I've always referred to the Bible and the scripture that speaks on love.

1 Corinthians 13:4-5 says, "Love is patient, love is kind. It does not envy, it does not boast, it is not proud. It does not

dishonor others, it is not self-seeking, it is not easily angered, it keeps no record of wrongs." We tell ourselves, if we really love someone, we should endure the pain because that makes us a 'ride-or-die,' someone who always has your back regardless of the situation, circumstances, or discomfort. Someone who chooses to endure suffering because that defines your loyalty and where you stand in the relationship. We are willing to give up anything, no matter the cost. We should forgive, even though cheating is a part of who he is. We let them curse and talk down to us because that's how he was raised, so we should understand.

Why do we equate love with pain? Why do we inflict hurt on ourselves, believing that going through hard times and enduring pain ensures that we indeed love that man? The question we should ask is, "How much do we love ourselves?" Why do we subject ourselves to a relationship with a man that doesn't value who we are? Hell, most men that mistreat women don't value themselves and that's the real problem. A man who inflicts pain on a woman is really hurting inside himself.

Everyone has heard the saying before, hurt people, hurt people and the truth is really just that simple. A man who abuses his woman in any form, struggles deep down inside with his own insecurities, trauma, and issues he has yet to deal with. The issue often has nothing to do with the woman but has everything to do with himself. People who don't accept or walk in their truth will only want the people around them to feel exactly how they feel on the inside. People who experience happiness only want to spread their happiness and impact others in a positive way; but some people who struggle with pain, past trauma, and unhappiness only want others to share that same pain.

Everyone has different coping mechanisms, but most men learn how to suppress their emotions while they are growing up. They suppress their tears when they hurt inside, they suppress their feelings when they can't deal with pain. And after all that suppressing, their pain will eventually come out in other ways of expression. Unfortunately, abuse is one of the main ways a man will express how he feels inside when he can't deal with past hurts in a healthy way. The pain that men endure honestly comes to a point where it becomes uncontrollable. Responding with abuse is something they feel they need to do in order to get their frustration out; it's a release for them. They need help and the woman who loves him unconditionally isn't the answer to his problem. I know you've heard the saying that most people hurt the person closest to them. Unfortunately, as their woman we become their punching bags. As much as we think we can fix a man and love him past his pain, we have to understand, he needs real help. Help that you aren't able to provide him.

For some women, when you understand the reasons why your man is abusive, you feel obligated to stand by his side, no matter what he puts you through. Some of the reasons are simply because you may share the same pain as he does. Or maybe you sympathize with him because of the trauma that he may have encountered. When you love someone, you never want to see that person hurt or going through pain. As women, we often try to love a man past his pain; we try to give him something he's never had or experienced before. You start to justify and make excuses for his behavior. You tell yourself because you love him,

79

you are supposed to stick it out with him. Being married or unmarried to a man should not be that much of a difference when you are being abused. Vows will cause you to fight and do all that you can to save your marriage, but so often, single women, who didn't say any vows, go through all of this hurt and pain for a man that isn't even their husbands! Married or not married, no one should have to endure *Abuse!*

God made women nurturers and believers. We hope for the best and we truly are loyal in love. Most women are very loyal and remain committed even through hardship. I can't count how many times my ex cheated on me but even when I left him, I still operated as if I was still with him. Even though I left, a big part of me still loved him and hoped he would one day change. Being with another man wasn't an option for me because I loved my ex and ultimately, he was who I wanted to be with. It's so easy to walk away but it's never easy to stay away! If I ever decided to be with another man while we were on a break, he would never have wanted to be with me again. Unfortunately, it's a double standard when it comes to how men deal with multiple women yet they are unwilling to accept when that same behavior is done to them.

Even though he called me names as if I slept around, he knew I wasn't going to deal with another man, even when we were broken up. This knowledge made him act a fool even more and he believed that no matter how many times he cheated or called me out by name, at the end of the day I wasn't going anywhere. A lot of men take women for granted, thinking we will always be around for them to treat us so unkindly, as if we don't deserve better. When I finally got the strength to leave for good, my daughter's father said to me "I never thought the day would come when you actually walk away from me." A lot of men want something from a woman that they can't even give us: loyalty. They want a loyal woman at home while they rip and run the streets. They have peace doing so because they know their woman is at home doing nothing but remaining true to them.

As years went by and I continued to be disrespected and cheated on, I started to lose more and more respect for him. Yet, I still respected myself enough to not to make an emotional decision or belittle myself by cheating in order to get back at him. All that my infidelity would have accomplished was to justify his own cheating, thinking I was disloyal the whole relationship. I knew that when I finally had the strength to leave him for good, I wanted to be able to say to myself that I was loyal, faithful, and loving towards him the entire time, despite how awfully he treated me. I was true to him and I never cheated on him. In his opinion, I spoke very disrespectfully to him but I only responded to him in the same manner he approached me with.

Despite my dedication to our relationship, I still started to lose respect for him as my man and even as a person. Once you lose respect for your man, there's no reason to stay in that relationship. Your connection will only become more and more toxic. When you've reached that point, ask yourself, "What am I really fighting for?" Let me answer that for you. Most of the time, we fight in the hope that he will one day change, that he will become the man he can potentially be, the potential you saw in him from the very beginning.

You have to admit that as women, we create a whole fantasy world in our heads instead of living in reality. We want that Prince Charming kind of man so badly that we convince ourselves that if we stick our relationship out, our man will become the prince we hope he is. Every woman is different and we all desire different qualities in a man. I'm going to be honest. I'm not going to say that I wanted a "bad boy" but I did want a man that could handle his own. Someone who could take control in situations and be all that I needed him to be when it came to his role as a man or a husband. People take "wanting a bad boy" out of context. We just want an Alpha Male, a man's man, not a man who allows anyone to run over them. Some women don't want a doormat that they can walk all over. A lot of women appreciate a man that makes us feel safe and protected, a man who takes control when needed, and a man who handles what needs to be managed. They respect our opinion as their women and they value who we are. There's nothing wrong with wanting certain characteristics you desire in a man, as long as those characteristics compliment you and allow you the growth to make you better as a woman.

Seeing the potential in a man often causes us to ignore his actions and not take them at face value. Some of you care too much about what others think. Others of you would rather suffer through abuse than to actually be alone. Instead, you must walk in your truth and deal with any insecurities that make you feel like you deserve less than you should. Being alone means more time to deal with your truth and anything you may need to change about yourself. Being in a relationship is hard work and it can also be used as a distraction.

Staying in a toxic, unhappy relationship really starts with you and how you view yourself. If you think you deserve better, eventually you will find the strength to leave. How we view ourselves is very important. If you don't think you are worthy of being happy and treated well, then being in a toxic, unhealthy relationship will most likely be where you think you belong. There are times when we don't know what hurts more: being alone and dealing with our very own pain or facing the pain that comes along with being in an abusive relationship. Unfortunately, for me the pain was too much to bear in that relationship. I was diagnosed with a heart condition because of our toxic relationship so I couldn't take the chance of continuing to hope and pray that he would one day be the man he could potentially be. Waiting on the potential of a man may mean you wait forever.

Please understand, you can find anyone on the street to mistreat you but it's hard to find a man that's going to choose to love you and respect you whether he is in your presence or not. Why do we stay in these dysfunctional relationships, acting as if we aren't worthy of being with someone that's going to treat us the way that we deserve? Is being alone really that difficult to deal with? Nothing is more difficult than being with a man who claims that he loves you but demonstrates behavior that only shows continuous disrespect toward you.

Let me be the one to tell you how worthy you are. You are a gem and you are so deserving to have God's best for your life. Being loyal to the wrong person can be so damaging. It is destructive to your spirit, your soul, and your self-esteem, and most importantly, harmful to your health.

Misplaced loyalty can even be detrimental to your children, as well as your family.

My brother never knew what took place in my relationship but he must have felt something was wrong because every chance he got, he voiced that he wanted me out of that relationship. The situation got so bad, I felt like I was in a position where I had to choose between my ex and my brother. It was horrible! I constantly argued with my brother KNOWING that my ex treated me awful, but feeling like I had to defend him. I fought with the people who truly loved me, all for a man I believed could potentially love me. My life was in *Shambles!*

Being diagnosed with a heart condition really put my life into perspective for me. I had to get to place and truthfully ask myself, "Is someone else's life more important than mine?"

I'll never forget the time I was at work in my shop and my daughters' father stopped by with two other people. He had already started drinking for the night, which was never a good situation. He got mad about something, pushed me against the wall, and started choking me. His two hands were gripped around my neck and I tried to break free but I couldn't breathe. Neither one of the people with him tried to stop him; they just wanted to mind their own business. Finally, he let me go, but if he had held on any longer it could have been the end for me; that's how hard he choked me.

Once I was free, the only reason why I didn't act a fool or try to fight him was because we were at my place of business. I just pictured what would happen if someone called the cops and with him already drinking; I knew he would get locked up and I didn't want that. So, what did I do? Absolutely nothing. The sad part about this incident is that I didn't even have a child with him at that time. So why did I feel the need to stay in that abuse? I justified that he choked me because he was drinking.

Whenever he drank, he was so quick to anger and violent and that wasn't with just me; that was how he behaved in general, with anyone. Without knowing why, I always blamed his abusive behavior on his drinking because most of the physical abuse came when he drank. I can only count on one hand how many times he's physically put his hands on me. Most of the abuse was verbal or emotional within the five years we were together. The last time he put his hands on me was when we were engaged and he got mad about something and he pushed my head. That's the day my son saw him slam me against the couch. I took my nails and scratched his face all up. That was my way of saying, "If you don't want your face messed up then learn to keep your hands to yourself." We didn't break up because at the time we were engaged. He went to work having to explain why he looked like he just got into a cat fight. I knew I couldn't beat him so I had to do something to make him think of his actions. It's so important to know your worth, or you will always find yourself in a place of emptiness and allow others to fill you up with their own substance of abuse.

Unfortunately, silent abuse isn't something that only women go through. I know there are some women who take advantage of the fact that their boyfriends, fiancés, or husbands won't put their hands on them. Then, they use that fact to their advantage. Ladies, you have to stop hitting and putting your hands on a man as well. You are an adult and you have to be able to control your anger without feeling the need to smack, punch, or hit your man just because you know he won't hit you back. You must do unto others the same way that you want done to you. If you continue to behave in that manner, you risk being hit back. So many men are abused by their women in silence yet they don't say anything because they don't want to seem weak. The same goes for same sex relationships. Expressing your emotions in an abusive way goes much deeper than the current circumstance that you face. We have to hold ourselves accountable in the same way we expect these men to do.

Silent abuse is real and there are so many women across this world who suffer from abuse without ever speaking out. Ladies, you are not alone, and if you want change or if you want to get out of your situation, you are going to have to speak up! No one deserves to be mistreated and abused. You deserve God's best for your life and a man who abuses you isn't who God intended for you to be with. Pray, and God will give you the strength and the resources to get out of your situation. But you have to walk in your truth and believe you deserve better!

Remember, how you choose to treat yourself, will always be the Standard of how you'll allow others to treat you.

Sex Ain't Better Than Love

Our heart is the most fragile part of the human body yet no one seems to handle it with care.

— Jenise McNair

Do we really believe as women that sex is better than love? No, but we definitely operate as if sex is better. Women often use the excuse they are trying to make their unhappy or dysfunctional relationship work because of their children. They want their children to have a Mommy and a Daddy in the same household. It's understandable that as a mother, you want your child to have the very best and to never go without. But that's not really the only reason why women try to hold on to the men who don't do right by them.

One of the main reasons, if not the most significant reason, why women stay in dysfunctional relationships is because the sex with that man is Good, Great, Awesome, Terrific, Outstanding, Tremendous, Refreshing... I can go on and on with words to describe Amazing Sex. I think it's safe to say most women have encountered this experience before. Through all the fussing, fighting, and cheating, somehow, some way, we just forget all the heartache once sex is involved. I'm sorry, I take that back. Not just 'sex' but *Great Sex*. Make-up sex is everyone's downfall because in the moment you forget about all the problems and issues at hand.

When a man makes love to you and makes you feel like you are on top of the world, you forget how this very same

87

person belittles you and makes you feel like nothing! Sex is so powerful, so endearing, so passionate, that it causes us to have cloudy judgment. One minute you're fed up with the fighting; the relationship is over, you're moving on. But the next minute you are rolling around telling that fool how much you love him, how you are all his, and how you aren't going anywhere! I'm laughing now but going through that vicious cycle sure wasn't funny back then. Having great sex chemistry can allow any toxic relationship to continue with no purpose, other than the feeling we chase in that 30 minutes of pleasure that amazing sex brings.

An unhappy woman will stay with her man for years just because she doesn't think there's another man out there that can make her feel the way he does in bed. Trust me, I've been there. I was twenty-three-years old and wet behind the ears when I met my daughters' father. He was eight years older than I was. He was sexually experienced and a man that took control in the bedroom. Right away, our sex chemistry was *amazing*!! Over time, throughout our relationship, my body just craved and yearned for his touch. Even from the very beginning of our relationship, we argued and disagreed so much that I now can look back on it and say we had no business being together. But the chemistry we had between each other, on top of our amazing sex, dumbed down situations that shouldn't have been overlooked. Sad to say, but sex had that much control over me.

Before kids were involved, there was still drama, still cheating, still abusiveness, and toxic, dysfunctional behavior that occurred. But I chose to overlook all of that all because of how he made me feel when he made love to me. Again, there were red flags from the very beginning when I should have walked away but I didn't want to leave everything behind, which included sex with him. I can't even say I stayed for our kids because a whole year went by before our first daughter was born. But in the midst of all the drama, the one thing that I could count on was the out-of-body experience I encountered anytime that man made love to me.

I was soul-tied to that man, my body yearned for his touch. No matter what pain he put me through, whether he cheated on me or disrespected me, having sex always was a temporary fix that I looked forward to. The sad part about the entire situation is that he made me feel so good when we made love, yet once that moment was over, he never made me feel good inside unless he was inside, literally! (Sorry, Dad, if you decided to read this chapter! I told you to skip it!) At the moment of realization that he took control in too many bedrooms other than mine, I had to keep it real with myself. How could I believe this man was for me, when the only time I felt like he loved me was when we made love? Every other moment in our relationship was all about him and what he wanted. Our relationship was never about me or trying to please me unless we were having sex. Then yes, I have to admit, he always made sure I came first -- literally.

But here's the kicker; I felt like the only good thing we had was sex, but to be honest, I didn't have that all to myself. He cheated every time he got mad at me. Not only did he cheat, but he had *unprotected* sex with these women, as if they were his women too. I couldn't believe his audacity. Not only did he cheat but he didn't protect himself either?

But remember, I said sex is powerful. So, I forgave him but I never forgot.

How could I forget the naked pictures in his camera, these chicks all over his bed? Naked. Bent over. I saw it all. So, as time went on, sex just wasn't enjoyable anymore. Every time he touched me, I could only think about him touching another woman in the same way. Every time he kissed me, I just pictured him kissing all the other women too. It got to a point that when we made love, I realized there was nothing special about what we had. Even though I was his woman, everyone else received the same benefits as I did.

The only thing that I had was the title of being his Woman and the headache that came with that 'privilege.' The other women got treated to dinner at all the restaurants that were our special places. Some even got invited to his home and slept in his bed. He even gave the same nickname to another female that he used to call me. I found that heartbreak in his phone while checking through his text messages. That awareness crushed me right there. All this time, I thought that was my special nickname. Nope! It was apparently multi-purposed.

"Honestly, what do you have with this man?" I asked myself. Nothing but a title that obviously meant absolutely nothing to him. A title that allowed me to be the woman he claimed and who he showed off to his family. When I told him I missed him, he said, "I miss you more!" But he said that to other women as well. I couldn't even have that small token of affection to myself. When I say I compromised everything as a woman, I compromised *everything*. And all for what? Thirty minutes of temporary pleasure that I was obviously sharing with others.

I realized I had to get my life together and I had to get it together fast. The fact that he put my health in danger and slept with other women unprotected, then came to sleep with me was just the ultimate disrespect and it was definitely unacceptable. He clearly didn't love me enough to want to protect me at all times. How could he say he loved me but risk giving me a STD because he had unprotected sex with other women? It was only by the grace of God, I never contracted anything. Even in the midst of his desire to sleep with other women, I couldn't understand why he didn't care about my well-being. Does this story sound familiar?

After I gave the engagement ring back to him and six months went by without us being together, I really thought our vicious cycle had finally come to an end. One day after going to court for child support, he expressed to me that he could have done things differently when we were engaged. I hadn't given the ring back because he cheated, I gave the ring back because he constantly kept coming in the house during hours that I felt were disrespectful. I thought when he proposed to me, he was ready to be a family man and he was finally going to put me first. But hanging out in the streets with his homeboys was more important to him. But that day, he expressed that he was wrong and he wanted to work on us.

I'm not going to lie. I genuinely loved that man and the thought of working on us again definitely crossed my mind. I wanted to believe that all those months apart really allowed him to think and change for the better. So of course, what did I do? I slept with him! But before I slept with him, I asked him one simple question, "I know you have been a single man for the past six months but did you have unprotected sex with anyone?" He responded, "No, I haven't." So, we reconciled our relationship. I missed him and he definitely missed me. We never went that long without each other before and I honestly felt like maybe this time would be different.

Then one day, we went through each other's phones, trying to prove to one another that we weren't hiding any secrets. I went straight to the photos. I didn't see anything until I decided to click on a blurry picture. It was video of him having unprotected sex with another woman. I instantly started yelling and going off! I asked him, "Why did you feel the need to lie to me and put my health in danger? If you would've just told me the truth you could've gotten tested or we could've just used a condom until you did. But you felt that lying to me was your only option." He mentioned that he met her at a bar and forgot all about that night because he was "drunk."

At that moment, I no longer wanted our relationship so badly that I would continue to be a fool for love. Nor would I continue to put my life on the line for a man who didn't value me or even himself. That was it for me. I couldn't do it anymore. I couldn't continue to allow this man to make me feel unloved and so unworthy. He wasn't honest with me because he couldn't be honest with himself. The summer of 2014, was the end of our vicious cycle. I could no longer justify his lies or his behavior to me. I could no longer choose to love this man more than I loved myself.

Does loving a man and enjoying sex cause you to compromise who you are, just for temporary pleasure? You may believe that because he makes you feel good when you two are making love, then it's okay to be mistreated outside of the bed. I finally had to realize that we never actually made love because outside of the bed, he didn't treat me with love. He treated me like I was his enemy, not the woman he said he wanted to spend the rest of his life with.

I used to tell him, "Leave me alone if you don't want me. If you want other women go have them." But he wouldn't leave me alone and even when we broke up, at some point, he came back, apologizing. Once again, I had to be honest with myself and ask. "Is Sex better than Love?" Not at all, especially if you're sharing your partner with everyone else. Are all relationships perfect? Not at all! No one's relationship is perfect but when two people respect each other, value each other, and don't take each other for granted, they can work through their problems.

Because of the relationship I endured, I learned a valuable lesson. Sex will never be able to hold two people together. Trust, respect, and loyalty are the foundations that every relationship should have. Your partner should love you enough to respect you; he shouldn't curse at you and call you degrading names just because he's mad at you. He should respect you enough to treat you how he wants to be treated. Loyalty means so much to me! If your man can't be loyal to you, then why even be in a committed relationship? Tell him to just stay single and live his life however he likes, with how ever many women he wants. Find a man that you can trust; no matter what you go through, he will always have your best interest at heart. Without trust, respect, and loyalty you have nothing but a dysfunctional relationship.

Mistaking passionate sex for love is normal for most women. A man should always show his display of love to you no matter what, even if he is mad or upset. Two years after I ended my vicious cycle with my daughters' father, I began a relationship with someone else. There were times when he was upset with me but he never disrespected me. He always showed me respect, despite the anger that he may have felt at the time. Being upset was never an excuse to belittle me or disrespect but instead, he always wanted to find a solution. Being angry doesn't give anyone a pass to be disrespectful or abusive. A man who loves you will only see you as his Queen, no matter what state of mind he is in.

Women often confuse anger with love. You think because he's going off, acting foolish, yelling, cursing, and fussing, that must mean he cares about you, right? No, his angry outburst means he's ignorant, immature, and doesn't know how to control his emotions. A man can be upset and frustrated without being disrespectful. If a man disrespects you, does that mean he doesn't love you? Unfortunately, we all have our own definition of love but I wasn't raised to disrespect the people I love. Respect should never be something that's only given based off your emotional stability; it should be on-going, no matter what! People say hurtful things they don't mean out of anger, but anger isn't an excuse to disrespect or say hurtful things to the person that you say you love.

In my first relationship after I decided to move on from my daughters' father, believe it or not, we never argued; we had our disagreements but we never fought. Even if we showed emotion or were both upset, he always allowed me to say how I felt without cutting me off. Then I did the same for him. He never cursed or yelled at me. Being upset never gave him an excuse to go out and cheat on me. He

94

wouldn't even allow me to go to bed upset. He wanted to come up with a solution right there at that moment before we went to bed. The maturity on his part as a man was so amazing, it was hard to remain angry with him.

Being in a relationship with him showed me it was possible to still be respected, loved, and cared for even when anger was present. The respect never went anywhere; he truly treated me as his Queen throughout the ups and the downs. You may ask, "So, where is he now?" He chose to walk in his truth and I had to respect and accept that. He realized he wasn't ready for the responsibility of dealing with a woman who had three kids. One minute he thought he was ready and the next minute he felt inadequate to deal with a woman with kids. Believe it or not, he was everything I needed and more. Again, I tried to build a man up instead of choosing one who understood how to build himself up. You can't want something so bad for someone if they don't want it bad enough for themselves. I could have kept him around until he figured it out and had sex with him regularly but I was at a point in my life when I wanted better and I knew better. I wanted more and I believed I deserved more than just *Amazing Sex!*

Ladies, sex before marriage isn't beneficial, especially with multiple people. You can't continue to let sex control your life, and you can't keep thinking that sex will bring you love. It won't, ladies, it just won't. Having sex with a man is not going to make him love you any more or less. Even if you just have sex for pleasure, you have to love yourself enough to stop sleeping with multiple men. Respect yourself enough to know that you deserve to be with someone who loves you for who you are. Having casual sex with just anybody is not healthy for you, emotionally or mentally. And if you want to get technical, sex may not be healthy for you physically either, especially if you don't protect yourself. Some of these men out here are complete *savages!* They act and then think later.

Previously, I talked about dealing with your "Truth." Dealing with your truth allows you to face the issues that are keeping you from growth or making wise decisions. If you sleep with multiple men because it makes you feel better, then I'm telling you that you are probably searching for an outlet that fills your void and it isn't what's inside a man's pants. You just use sleeping around as a way to cope and suppress whatever it is in your life that you are struggling with. Ladies, I'm not judging you at all. Trust me, I understand how dealing with your past can open up wounds that you aren't ready to confront. But sleeping around with different men only causes you to create another wound that you will have to address later on.

Nothing feels better than a man who can love you unconditionally, without expecting you to open your legs for him. A man who loves you because of who you are. One who realizes that spending time with you is more than enough. But nothing is greater than loving yourself first and knowing your own self-worth.

Sex was designed to be an added benefit to a marriage. Sex was supposed to come after the vows, after you already fell in love with your spouse. But society and our flesh caused us to believe that sex is the be-all, end-all. As if sex is what defines a person. No Ladies, sex doesn't define you. Your heart, your character, and your integrity are what defines you, not what's between your legs. But the truth is, the right man will look for all of those qualities in you first. I know that idea may sound crazy, but honestly, a real man can appreciate a woman's presence that brings nothing but joy and laughter that truly touches his soul. A lesser man can only appreciate bending you over. Having good chemistry, smiles, good conversation, and respect can go a long way and develop into a healthy relationship and one day, even marriage.

Stop allowing sex to control you! Stop allowing society to make you feel like if you aren't having sex, then no man is going to give you the time of day. As a matter of fact, inform every man you meet that you aren't having sex, just so you can get rid of the idiots. You don't want the type of man who's only looking for sex anyway.

Ladies, we are so much more than what we have between our legs. We don't realize how much power we hold, how much control we really have. In the song, "This is a Man's World" by James Brown, he sings, "This is a man's world BUT it wouldn't be nothing, nothing without a woman or a girl." Those lyrics clearly state, yes, men are in the forefront but it's the women who are really running the show. When it comes to dating, a man can't do anything without the woman's permission. Although we are often underappreciated and treated so unfairly, we truly are an asset to men and to this world in general.

We make it so easy for men to slack off and get out of properly courting women like they should. On the first date, we sleep with them; on Instagram, we expose everything, leaving no need for imagination. If you don't sleep with them, they don't care because the next female will. But that casual view of sex is the problem.

More women need to take control of their bodies and understand that their self-worth is so much greater than sleeping around for attention or to feel needed. I used to say to myself often, "I wish I had my virginity back!" If we gained back control over our lives, over our bodies and demanded to be courted and respected, men would have to fall in line. Men don't court women because they don't have to anymore. Sex is just thrown at them without even asking and the world we live in promotes nothing but SEX, SEX, and MORE SEX. All you hear today is "sex sells." Yeah, sex sells alright, it sells your soul.

For every man you sleep with, you are soul-tied to that man. This idea means that you are connected with someone even if you no longer want to be. Think about it on spiritual level; sex was created for husband and wife to become one once they are married. When two people have sex, life can be created. So how can we not think sex isn't just as powerful outside of marriage? Why do we feel as though when we sleep with someone those connections and bonds aren't formed? Sex is powerful and we have to stop allowing it to have so much control over our lives and our choices.

Do you know how precious you are? Do you know how worthy you are? Despite your past, despite your problems, you are still worth more than you think you are. I know breaking unhealthy habits that aren't beneficial to you may be hard, but choosing to do things differently will change your life for the better. Choosing to be patient and not having casual sex with just anyone will allow you have control over your emotions and feelings. Taking your time to get to know someone before having sex will allow you to avoid later disappointments about that man you aren't willing to deal with. Truly having self-control means you won't allow your body to crave a man sexually based on his looks or actually act on those temptations.

I tell my coaching clients all the time that I'm not asking you to do anything I haven't done. Even though I didn't have multiple men that I slept with, that one man still had a hold on me. I just couldn't walk away. I even tried to convince myself that maybe I could break up with him but still sleep with him since he was the father of my daughters. Sex will hold you captive in situations and make you feel like you can't escape. How can someone make you feel so good but cause you so much pain?

We, as women, can't worry about all the other women in the world. All we can do is hold ourselves accountable and better ourselves. Taking the time to work on you from the inside out will allow you to build your own self-worth, one day at a time. Find positive and healthy hobbies you enjoy that add to your life instead of giving a part of yourself to a man that doesn't deserve you. Take yourself out of the equation when it comes to sleeping around with men just because it feels good. Just because something tastes good or feels good doesn't mean it's good for you. Sex isn't going anywhere; But being with someone who truly loves you, for more than what's between your legs, now that's something *special*. It's wonderful when you find someone who values and respects you. But you must love, respect, and value yourself first, before expecting these qualities from anyone else.

Do you allow sex to control your life and decisions when it comes to men? Have you invested too much of yourself without first finding out if this relationship is a good investment or not? It is time for you to change your thought process when it comes to dating and dealing with the men you meet from this day forward. Every time you find yourself about to make a bad investment, just ask yourself, "Is making this permanent decision based off a temporary circumstance a good investment of my self-worth?" If you want something you have never had, you must be willing to do something you have never done before.

Remember, how you choose to treat yourself will always be the Standard of how you'll allow others to treat you.

The Second Option

I want to have my cake and another cake too,
even if the baker don't bake like you;
even when the flavor don't taste like you.

— J. Cole

The Second Option: a woman chosen by a man who already has other obligations and commitments to another woman.

Side chicks, mistresses, or "the other woman" are what the world calls them but I believe the second women chosen by men aren't any of those elements. They are just the second option to men who put themselves in a compromising position, so that they can have their cake and eat it too. This topic is a very sensitive subject for a lot of women. So many women, wives, and children have been hurt and affected in some form or fashion when it comes to the second option. This topic isn't spoken about in church but is a prevalent problem in today's world. There are so many women who become the other woman by choice, while others don't realize they are the second option until it's too late. It's very easy to pass judgment on these women when you aren't in their shoes.

We are all human and we all make mistakes at some point in our lives. Yet, even within our mistakes we still should hold ourselves accountable. Again, some women are oblivious to being the second option while other women prefer being the second option. Some women even become the second option simply by trying to be a friend. I used to frown upon any woman who carried on with a man who

101

was taken. God allowed me to go through a situation in order to show me how easy it is to do what you said you would never do. So, who am I to pass judgment on anyone?

This book is all about being transparent and showing women that no matter what you subject yourself to in life that you may regret later, it is possible to overcome anything and everything. *We aren't always given a second chance to right our wrongs but if you are presented with that opportunity, choose to do what's right.*

As a mother of three, my life was always hectic. I worked two or three jobs, dropped off, picked up, worked out, or just did errands for my kids. I never really had time to go out and mingle or meet new people. If I had the time, I was too tired to do anything and I preferred to stay in the house and lay low.

On one rare occasion, an old friend had a birthday party in DC and my cousin and I decided to go. Keep in mind, it took me forever to get dressed because a part of me didn't feel like going. By the time I forced myself to get ready, it was already six o'clock and the party ended at eight. I figured I would still show my face and go even though it was almost over.

When we arrived at the party, my cousin and I looked at each and clearly thought, "We are definitely over-dressed." But we knew we weren't staying long so it didn't matter. We were there for about 15 minutes, when I spoke to my friend and he got us a drink. I noticed a guy by the door in my peripheral vision but never made eye contact. As I danced, I felt someone close to me, then out of nowhere, the guy swipes and hits my arm. I gave him a look of, "Why are you touching me?"

He quickly responded to my look and said, "I'm sorry you had a bug on you!"

Now I am terrified of bugs so I instantly felt like I should listen to whatever he had to say. I started laughing and asked him, "Was it really a bug or did you just want to see if my skin was really as soft as it looked?"

He responded, smiling, "For real, there was a bug on you."

Of course, you already know what came next! He asked me if I had a boyfriend. I normally say yes to alleviate any extra conversation but again, I felt like I owed him the truth so I responded "No!"

He said, "You are lying. There's no way you are single."

Now listen, I'm not new to this game, the father of my daughters schooled me. He may have hurt me but his actions taught me a lot when it comes down to men who are deceitful. So, I asked him, "What's your story? You got a girl, wife, complicationship, or situationship? Which one?"

He laughed and said, "None of the above. I have a sonship. I have two boys, that's it. Oh, and I'm divorced."

Instantly, I said to myself, "Divorce? Oh no. He's definitely not getting my number!" But a voice in my head said, "Stop it Jenise. Just see what he's about!"

He later whispered in my cousin's ear that I would one day be his girlfriend. He seemed to be a very confident man and secure within himself. He wasn't really my type but he was still attractive. I had to remind myself that focusing on looks is what caused me the most drama in the past so I should do something different.

When we got ready to leave, there were some steps we had to go down. As I proceeded to go down the steps and he yelled out, "You don't see my hand? Let me help you down these steps."

As I laughed, he commented, "You aren't used to a man being a gentleman."

"There aren't many of those out there, anymore," I replied. He helped my cousin and me down the stairs, then he walked me to my car.

He texted me later that night and we talked. He told me his family was from the area but he lived two hours away in Virginia with his sons. He mentioned to me he moved there to be closer to his sons because that's where his ex-wife relocated once they got a divorce. He also mentioned he came up to DC every weekend because his friends and family lived nearby. I believed it wouldn't hurt to get to know him because he didn't even live in the area.

As time went on, we started talking every day. All day, every day. He always made me a part of his day in some way. I started to like him a lot and I fell in love with who he was as a father to his sons. I really respected his level of commitment and the effort he made towards being a father. I was often on the phone with him when he picked up his sons from school and practice or while doing homework with them at night.

He frequently came into town on the weekends, which worked for me because I was busy during the week. Being long-distance actually worked for us until I realized the weekends weren't enough. I wanted to see him more. He invited me out of town one weekend and he was the perfect gentleman the entire time. He was a really nice guy. That's how I described him to my friends.

He mentioned to me that he and his ex-wife had a good co-parenting relationship. I admired this fact but I also knew if we ever got serious, some details would have to be adjusted. He mentioned I was the first woman he pursued since his divorce, even though he had been divorced for two years. Getting back in the dating scene was new to him after being married for eleven years.

As time went on, the distance between our homes started to bother me. I wondered where exactly this relationship was going. My time was precious and I didn't want to waste time or guess where I stood in someone's life. I met with him to tell him that the long distance wasn't going to work out after all. I told him that we should cut our losses before our situation got any more serious. As nice as it was to have someone to talk to or FaceTime with every day, I knew that kind of relationship wasn't enough for me. But I didn't think he would be able to give me more due to the distance.

After our conversation, he came up one weekend and asked me to give him more time because he didn't want to lose me. I felt like he was genuine and sincere so I agreed to give him the two weeks he asked for, before making the decision to part ways permanently. Of course, we fell back into our routine of talking and Facetiming all day, every day. But I still felt uneasy about where we were in our situationship. A part of me felt like he just wanted to go for the ride and see where we ended up, but I wasn't willing to ride without knowing exactly where the relationship was going. He felt that I was distancing myself and asked me to be patient to give him some more time. He mentioned that he wouldn't be able to visit every weekend as in previous months because of his sons' sport schedules and everything else he had going on in his life.

Something just didn't feel right and my woman's institution started to speak to me. Six weeks went by without seeing each other and I couldn't understand how that was okay for him. So, I became a 'private investigator' to look for information that might explain his excuses for not visiting. We never think that the worst could happen until that situation happens to us. As much as he was a great guy, a respectful gentleman, and a terrific father, it turned out that he was also still *someone else's husband*!

I just couldn't believe that he lied about being married! Regardless of his reasoning, I still wanted to hold him accountable for his lie and I felt like he owed me an explanation. I didn't know what to think; I was so hurt and I couldn't believe that I had become someone's second option. Luckily, I was at a different place in my life so I knew that yelling, fussing, and cursing weren't going to help me understand the situation. I really wanted to hear what his thought process was. You see, circumstances like this may happen all the time on television or with someone you know, but let me tell you, this situation definitely hits differently when it happens to you!

I stayed calm even when I spoke to him later that evening. He acted perfectly normal and I tried my hardest not to say anything. I could've confronted him over the phone but that would've bailed him out. He could've hung up or blocked me if I had chosen to have the conversation over the phone. But I wanted to approach him in person. I wanted to see that stupid look on his face when I exposed his lies. He mentioned that he was coming up Saturday, so I had to play it cool for three days. That was a long three days, borderline torture. But believe it or not, I made it through the three days without giving any hint that something was wrong.

When he arrived, he immediately told me how much he missed me, using all his acting skills. You know, a lot of cheating and deceitful men are actors and they truly get into character. He hugged me tight and held me close, telling me how much he missed me. And I whispered in his ear, "You miss me like you miss your wife?"

He immediately jumped back and looked at me with the exact stupid look on his face I envisioned. "You are still married, right?" I asked as I showed him the proof and evidence I found.

He looked at me with shame and said, "I wanted to tell you but I got in too deep. By the time I realized what an amazing woman you were, I knew that I would lose you if I told you I was married. So, I lied because I chose to be selfish instead of doing the right thing."

I asked him, "How long did you think this relationship was going to last? My expectations of what we could be would only grow over time." But he honestly didn't know how long he was going to continue to lie.

"Until you got caught." I said, "That sounds about right!"

I don't know if he was more shocked with how calm I was or the fact I found out. I asked him, "Why are you out here living a lie?"

He admitted that he was unhappy and his marriage was falling apart. He never wanted a divorce because of the drama that came with one and he believed it was best to stay with his wife for their kids.

I looked at him and retorted, "You have two boys and is this role model you want to give your sons?"

He told me how happy I made him and how he sacrificed his happiness for so long.

But I replied, "That doesn't justify your poor behavior as a husband, a man, or a father! Your selfish decisions unfortunately don't just affect you. They affect the people you love as well. This poor choice you made affects your children, your marriage, and how others will choose to view your character."

He apologized and then had the nerve to ask me if I would wait for him to get a divorce.

"No," I told him, "What makes you think I would want to be with a man like you after you lied to me all this time?"

At that point, I knew he wondered what my next move would be. I could tell he was still waiting for me to go off, hitting him and acting crazy. But I didn't allow myself to give that much energy to him. Instead I wanted him to hear me and I wanted him to hear me clearly. I told him, "I have your wife's cell phone number and I know where you live, but luckily for you, I have no desire to hurt her or to put your family through the pain I know this will cause, if I choose to contact your wife."

"So, I guess I'll never see or hear from you again," he said, disappointed.

I responded, "You guessed correctly."

In that very moment, I finally understood why women choose to stay in a situation with someone who is married until it sorts itself out, if it ever does. After six months of talking every day, spending time together on the weekends and getting to know one another, I missed him. Even though he lied, I still believed he was a good person who just made a selfish decision. Men and women find themselves in these predicaments all the time. It might seem so easy to say what you would choose to do until you find yourself in that same place.

Here's the truth about my situation, I'm still human and even though I found out he was married, my feelings for him did not just disappear immediately. They didn't develop quickly and they weren't going to fade instantly either. Finding out the truth didn't mean the next day I didn't look for his call or his text. I missed our connection.

I always try to put myself in the other person's shoes. I recognize that there are so many marriages and relationships where people are unhappy. When people feel stuck in their situations, they get desperate and seek happiness elsewhere. Even though he lied to me and deceived me, I still believe he was really a good person who made a very poor decision. We had great chemistry together and unfortunately, I couldn't change the fact that I developed feelings for someone else's husband. Yikes! I finally understood why it's so hard for women who become involved in relationships with married men, to just walk away.

I never got to a place where I fell in love with him but I kept asking myself, what if I had? I'm honestly not sure that I would have been able to walk away so easily if I had allowed myself to love him. Luckily, I was in a place in my life where I knew who I was and I knew what I wanted. I knew being someone's second option wasn't what I deserved nor was that God's plan for me.

The temptation that our flesh craves is so strong. As women we are emotional beings, so it's not easy for most women who fall in love with a married man to feel as if they can really walk away and cut all ties. Some women may even feel like they've been mistreated all their lives, so when they finally find a man who treats them special or like a queen, even if he is married, walking away from that special bond becomes very difficult.

I was truly blessed to be where I was in my life because I could have easily allowed my feelings for him to trap me in a position where I didn't belong. As much as I missed him, as much as I wanted to try and convince myself we could stay in contact, I knew better. Emotions were already involved on both ends, so staying in contact wouldn't have been smart on my part. I knew I deserved better. Every woman deserves to be a man's *only* option but we shouldn't be willing to hurt another woman to become a man's *only* option either. Period.

When love is a factor, it's not easy to walk away from a deep connection, married or not. When money or material items are considerations, it's not easy to walk away, especially if money is important to you. Some of these married men spoil their second options, buying them whatever they want and treating them like queens. They take them on trips and pay their bills. The guy that was married always communicated that he didn't want me to entertain anyone else. There he was with a wife at home, making demands on me. These married men are still very possessive and territorial when it comes to their second option.

Unfortunately, we live in a world today where we make a lot of decisions based off how we feel rather than what's right. Let's just be honest. Women who make a conscious decision to continue their relationships with married men clearly make that choice based off their own personal feelings and desires, not off the reality that he is a married man. Many women find themselves in similar situations to mine. They fall in love with men who are married or in a committed relationship but did not know that these men weren't available from the very beginning. These women aren't just "side chicks" because these men choose to treat these women, as if they are the only option. They give these women the same amount of respect, time, money, energy, arguments, babies, and investments as if these women were their wives or girlfriends. These men fall in love with their second option and they allow themselves to get in too deep. Some men have no intention of leaving their wives or their second option. And as we all know, some men actually leave their wives for their second option.

Back in the day, side chicks were just that: side chicks. The men made it very clear that they would never come first, so they weren't to come in between him and his family. He would never leave his wife, so don't ever ask. The relationship was basically just sex, an outlet when his wife got on his nerves. Now, these men literally live a double life. Two wives or two girlfriends with two families, trying to juggle it all.

Some women know the truth but many women have been lied to for years. Some men are really that good at juggling all the aspects of living a double life until they get caught. These women are chosen as their man's "second option." Temptation gets the best of a lot of men, causing them to risk everything. I'm sure some of these men wish they met their second option before they met their wives. Simply because every woman is different, he may enjoy his second option better than his first. By the time these men realize that they've fallen for someone other than their "first option," there's too much time invested and these men honestly feel like they cannot live without that new woman. Unfortunately, this investment causes some men to leave their families and divorce their wives. The second option now becomes the new first option.

I believe that when most men have sex with women, it's just sex to them; a physical act, nothing more, nothing less. Women place a deeper meaning on sex than men. We are emotional beings and most of the time we have sex based on our feelings and that intimacy causes us to have an emotional connection to that man. Men can have sex with very little emotional connection at all. Between temptation and curiosity, visualizing having sex with a woman whom they are attracted to often causes them to make poor choices. Men will risk everything, their marriages, their children, or their stability, just for thirty minutes of a sexual act. If men don't have enough self-control to fight temptation, then they don't belong in a relationship or marriage because they won't remain faithful.

I respect a man who admits he loves women too much to commit to just one. That may be his truth and there's absolutely nothing wrong with that! Every woman has a choice, if we choose to have sex with a man who clearly communicates that he's single because he loves women that much, then that's our mistake. We shouldn't entertain the men with this type of mindset on any sexual level. Many relationship issues could be avoided if people just choose to accept and walk in their truth. We must understand that all men or women aren't *marriage material!* There's many men and women who don't desire to be married.

People stay in marriages and relationships because of time invested, kids, money, shared assets, or just pressure from friends and family. The sad part is, no one factors in their very own happiness. An unhappy person in a marriage or a relationship will, at some point, seek happiness somewhere else. The other person doesn't make them happy anymore so they seek out someone who does. Over time, people in relationships begin to go through the motions and become a little more than roommates. In my opinion, marriage isn't set up for people who may grow apart later.

There's plenty of couples who have been married for over 30 years but when their children go off to college, they get a divorce. It's like they think, "Hey the kids are eighteen now and out of the house, we can finally be free and happy!" They were so busy raising kids and working that their fire for each other died down. The problem isn't that the fire died down, the problem comes when no one wants to rekindle the love. It's sad that most people value their image or what others may think more than they value their own happiness. People stay married for their children, believing togetherness is for the best. But children know when their parents aren't happy and that decision is not always the best choice.

Ladies, regardless of your past, regardless of your current circumstances, I want you to know that you are worth being someone's *only* option and nothing less than that. A man has a choice to love you and be with only you. If he can't give you that requirement, love yourself enough to know you deserve better.

There was a time when I found out my daughters father was cheating with another woman while we were together. As crazy as it sounds, I felt so bad for the other woman! Forget about my feelings and the fact that my man lied to me. Based on her text messages to him, she was in love with my man. She wanted a family and a future with him. I felt sorry for her because I knew, even though he treated me like trash, there was a part of him that didn't want to live without me. When I confronted her, she said to me, "Now I know why he won't move forward with me. It's because his heart is still with you."

A year later, when he proposed to me, I thought about her because I knew she saw the engagement post on social media. I didn't know her personally but based off our conversation, I felt that she was a good person and just got caught up, which is so easy to do. Unfortunately, she put her heart on the line for someone who had no intention to handle her heart with care. As a woman, I was able to empathize with her and I was truly sorry she experienced the pain he caused her.

I do believe some women are really oblivious when a man is not being honest. I wasn't aware myself of any lies until I found out I was dating a married man. I realize that no matter how small or big a red flag may be, it is always important to communicate and get clarity on anything that makes you feel uneasy. That one small red flag you ignore or overlook can lead to a *big disappointment!*

We must learn how to love ourselves, build ourselves up, and truly figure out who we are so that we never feel like we have to accept less than what we deserve. As women, we have to believe and know our own self-worth so we do not fall prey to situations that take away from who we are meant to be. Our flesh and our feelings toward temptation are strong, so knowing our own self-worth and what we deserve has to be much stronger. You gain this strength when you are tired of the vicious cycle and you know that you want more for yourself.

We must stop expecting others to give us what we can give ourselves, *true happiness.* We should always make sure we can give ourselves everything that we need. If not, we will always be in bondage to what others can do for us. We should place ourselves in a position where we can fulfill responsibilities for ourselves, whether it's paying our own bills, treating ourselves to something nice, or taking a relaxing vacation to get away.

At the end of the day, how we choose to handle dating is really based off how we choose to handle ourselves. Being the 'second option' should never be your choice because queens deserve to be the *Only Option* but not at the expense of hurting another woman.

Now, ask yourself, "Am I settling for far less than I deserve?" Do you still beat yourself up about a poor relationship decision you made in your past that you regret? Forgive yourself and learn how to push forward. Take

115

ownership and accountability, then choose to move forward in a different direction. Please understand, Ladies, it's never too late to try and do what's right, especially if there's still an opportunity to still do so.

Remember, how you choose to treat yourself will always be the Standard of how you'll allow others to treat you; or better yet, how you choose to treat others.

Game Changer

And since we all came from a woman;

Got our name from a woman and our game from a woman.

— Tupac Shakur

Everyone you date has potential but that potential doesn't necessarily mean they will want to become what you see in them, especially if they don't see those same possibilities in themselves. We invest our time, energy, money, and emotions into the potential of someone who may never become what we hope and believe they could be.

Every person should be honest with where they are in life, especially when it comes to dating. There's nothing wrong with a single man weighing his options, as long as he's not deceitful in the process. Every woman should know who she is and not allow herself to do anything she can't handle emotionally or will regret later on. If you aren't a woman who can handle having casual sex without getting emotionally involved, then the temporary pleasure isn't worth the emotional hardship that comes later. The pleasure that we get from having great sex for that short amount of time isn't worth the long-lasting heartache we feel while trying to figure out what role we play in a man's life. Trying to understand where a man prioritizes you in his life is a terrible feeling, especially when that man should make sure you know exactly what role you play in his life, if you are important to him.

When I was a child, I spoke as a child, I understood as a child, I thought as a child; but when I became a man, I put away childish things. — 1 Corinthians 13:11

This verse should be every woman's favorite scripture in the Bible when it comes to dating because we can truly appreciate when a man has finally reached a point in his life when he knows who he is and what he wants out of life. He's done with the childish games and he chooses to operate and represent himself as a real man. Some guys grow up a lot sooner than others, and some don't grow up at all.

A strong indication that you are dealing with a grown boy is his inability to be honest. Honesty alone goes a long way in any type of relationship. When a man is upfront with you about where he is in life and what he is looking for in a relationship, then it's up to you to make a decision on whether or not he's someone you want to continue dealing with. If a man told you he's not looking for a commitment, or he's seeing other women, or he doesn't see marriage in his future, you have to take what he said at face value. Don't try to alter what he said to fit whatever it is that you are looking for in a relationship or in a man.

The greatest gift God gives us in life is the ability to choose. We have the power and control to make any choices we desire pertaining to our lives. Many men are totally upfront with women yet these women totally disregard their honesty because they think that in time, he will change his mind. Once you've reached a certain age, playing the guessing game shouldn't even exist. If both men and women are straightforward and state what they want from the beginning, the games should be eliminated.

If a man is dating to have fun and a woman is dating to have fun, then there really shouldn't be any problems. But things seem to get complicated when someone isn't honest with the other person or honest with themselves. If you're dating to settle down and get married, then you shouldn't entertain a man who's dating just to have fun. And most importantly, you shouldn't date, expecting to change his mind. Respecting a man's honesty should really be that simple.

But of course, if he's attractive, then we often make exceptions, even though we knew we were supposed to leave him alone from the beginning. Our eyes are the gateway that leads us down a road of destruction. The attractiveness of a woman causes a man to forget, in that moment, that he's got a baby on the way, he's in a relationship, or even that he has a wife and kids at home. The attractiveness of a man causes a woman to downplay the fact he's grown but still lives at home with his mother, he doesn't spend time with his kids, he's married even if he's unhappy, or he simply doesn't even have a reliable vehicle.

Ladies, there is a lot of truth to the saying, "Every man is different but the game don't change." Men play games, women play games, we are all guilty of playing games. But as women, we put up with a whole lot more than what most men are willing to deal with. Most of the time, a man shows signs of playing games early on but we choose to ignore them. What is it about a man, especially the ones that are *fine,* that cause us to forget what we deserve or how we should be treated? Why do we as women allow ourselves to get so wrapped up with a man who's not even willing to make a commitment? Perhaps, you go on dates to get to know each other and you enjoy each other's company. He gives you time but he won't give you a commitment. Why? Because without the commitment, he can justify seeing other women! This is just another game that men play; stringing you along and giving you what you want to hear just to keep you around.

Unfortunately, a man isn't wrong for handling himself in that manner because you allowed him to lead you on and leave you in a space of uncertainty. He's not your man, but you still choose to sleep with him. That's where we lose our power and lose control of our emotions. If he's not your man, then why do you treat him as if he is? Why do you cut everyone off for him when he hasn't done the same for you? We get so caught up in being with a man that we expect too much from someone that we are supposed to just be dating. What's wrong with dating a man, getting to know him, and keeping sex out of the equation? There's nothing wrong with a man who tells you that he's not ready for a committed relationship. Actually, you should be glad that he's honest and straight-forward with you. At least you know where he stands from the beginning. It's important that we take what a man says at face value pertaining to where he stands in his life.

But here's where the problem comes into play. When he tells you that information, you choose to ignore it, try to convince yourself that you're okay with it, or think that in time, he will change his mind. He may give you the time, and he may even communicate with you on a regular basis, but he won't give you the commitment that you want. For those of you who aren't okay with not being in a committed relationship, why would you sleep with someone who isn't your man, when you already know what the end result will be?

Let's be honest here. Once you have sex with a man who you feel has potential, you automatically develop feelings and set expectations that he has no intention of ever meeting. So, what is the next step? What is your game plan? Operating as if you can change him means you are headed down the road of emotional suicide! As women, we can't help how we feel about someone, especially when we add physical intimacy in the mix. We have to stop making permanent decisions based on temporary circumstances. We are not doing justice to ourselves, Ladies.

I talked to a guy years ago (this was before I met the married guy) and we really had good vibes around each other. We had a lot in common and I enjoyed hanging out with him. We talked on the phone, FaceTimed each other, and texted all day long. We talked about serious matters, like what he was looking for in a relationship and where he was at that point in his life. He conveyed to me that he liked me and that he wanted to continue getting to know me. On any given night, he asked me what I was doing. One evening, I told him I planned to go running. He offered to meet me in downtown DC to run a couple of miles with me. He was not a runner but he just wanted to be around me, so he was a runner that night! Believe it or not, he did really well and actually ran four miles that night!

Ladies, trust me, if a guy really likes you, he will be willing to do a lot of things that are out of his comfort zone just to be in your presence. Can you imagine this guy going running with a woman who runs marathons for fun? The whole time he tried to hold his own as a man and make sure he didn't die at the same time. Honestly, he got big brownie points that night; he impressed himself and me. We just ran and carried on a conversation, laughing and getting to know one another. I mean, running with a man who you're interested in, knowing you will sweat and your hair will be all messed up is a Big Deal. The old me would have never allowed myself to be that vulnerable, but running is a big part of who I am. Being transparent and showing him or anybody else the sweaty, messy version of myself is important to me.

As women, we really should get to a place in our lives where we can always be ourselves and not care about what other people think. Being true to yourself means embracing everything about yourself, whether it's the good or the bad. You'll get to this place when you choose to live for you and no one else. Focusing only on the things that make you better and make you happy. What you think of yourself is what matters most, not the opinion of others. I continued to talk to this guy as the days and weeks went on. Most of our dates were pretty chill. We met up at the bar to have some drinks or we spent time together on Saturday nights. We both were flexible about making time to try and connect with each other.

But then, our connection got a little bit tricky. The more time you spend with someone, the more your feelings get involved and the more you feel invested in that person. The world that we live in seems so big, but to some degree, it is really so small when you start dating. I mentioned to my friends about how I was having a good time with him and then Bam! He knows somebody, who knows somebody, that knows somebody.

When circumstances seem too good to be true, most of the time, they are. I found out through mutual friends that he was in a 'situationship.' He denied that he was in a relationship but he was involved with someone else, so I'm just going to call it a situationship. When we met, I did ask him if he had a girlfriend but what I didn't ask him was if he had a situationship. I guess that was my fault. In this day and time, you have to ask very specific questions or they will be able to say, "You never asked me!" You know, the "don't-ask-don't-tell" concept.

Men often find themselves in relationships where they aren't happy but they aren't man enough to get out of those situations for whatever reason. They get complacent, the living arrangements are complicated, or there are kids involved. But their reason for staying becomes a big mess when they decide to go out as if they are single or free of any complications in their lives and then try to meet another woman.

I approached him and asked about the situation in a calm and open-minded manner. I allowed him to have his say and we discussed the information like adults. Let me be honest, if I had made a decision to have sex with him already, then clearly that conversation would've been much different. My emotions would have gotten in the way and not allowed me to be calm enough to really talk like adults. I believe that sex just takes your mindset and your feelings to a whole other level when dealing with someone you date.

After three kids and two baby daddies, at this point in my life, I am not trying to make poor decisions that will hurt me in the long run. I didn't feel as invested in this man

123

because I chose to not have sex with him. Being older and wiser, I was able to act smart about the situation. We make too many bad investments in men that never end up with a good return. At some point we have to start to make decisions differently.

Because I was not as emotionally invested in my date as I could have been, I was more of a disappointed friend to him than an "angry black woman." So, we talked and he conveyed to me, he wasn't happy but he was content being in his situationship because it was familiar. Men normally play a back-and-forth game; they want to break up to make up. When there's nothing going on right now at the moment, they tolerate their woman since she's around and not going anywhere. That's how his situationship with the other woman operated. I told him who wants to live like that? Of course, he mentioned when he met me, he started to like me and didn't want to say anything about his situationship.

Don't ask me why I am such a nice person but I am. In that moment, I simply became his friend and took myself out of the shoes of being a woman he was interested in. I instantly felt like I needed to use this time to really make him understand that stringing the other woman along wasn't cool. It wasn't fair to him or to her to keep a connection going that was no longer there. She believed and hoped for a future with him and he stayed, which made her think he was happy and might marry her one day. When you've been with someone for a long time and the fire dies, it is hard to let go, especially when you don't want to hurt the other person's feelings. I told him, "If I was her, I would've left you. All those years (more than ten years) with her and you haven't even considered marriage." I told him to let her

124

go, so she could find the person who wanted her just as much as she wanted him. He needed to stop wasting her time and his, as well as the time of other women who met him and thought he was available. He needed to go get himself together, focus on making a change, and do what he needed to do as a man.

We are friends on social media so we keep in touch here and there. From my understanding, he followed my advice and got out of his situationship. I honestly believe that the men who find themselves in these compromising situations aren't necessarily bad people. Some men, okay, a lot of men, just don't think about their circumstances. Guys really have to do a better job of handling relationships and using their brains. Men aren't stupid, they just don't think through the consequences whenever it involves situations dealing with females. They instantly become selfish and just want whatever they see, without factoring in their current situation.

We all make mistakes and poor decisions. I obviously met him for a reason, so I allowed God to use me at that moment in time to encourage him to improve and start making better decisions. I knew he was a good person; he came from a good home. He was still just trying to find his way as a man. There's no reason to beat a brother while he's down. You really do need to kill people with kindness. Later he even thanked me for confronting him face-to-face. I appreciated that he was man enough to meet with me and recognize where he went wrong.

Honestly, the game that men and women play really doesn't change, Ladies. You just always have to be a couple of plays ahead. Don't play checkers, play *chess!*

125

Dating nowadays is extremely different; mostly because a lot of men just aren't honest. Men are always going to want what they want without considering where they are in life. A man meets a woman knowing he's not available but somewhere in his brain he thinks, "Just get her number anyway. You can figure all that other stuff out later." Yet the game just doesn't play out the way they want it to play out. Men are very visual. They see an attractive woman and often lose sight of what is important. Right at that moment, they forget they have a girlfriend, a baby mama, or even a wife at home with their kids.

Is it possible for a man to have his cake and eat it too, with one woman? Absolutely, once he's figured out what cake and flavor hits the spot. He has to choose a cake he doesn't mind eating over and over again. It's like your favorite food. I, personally, never get tired of eating crab and shrimp; I feel joy just thinking about eating them. That's how a man should feel when he's found the right woman.

J. Cole in his song "Kevin's Heart," wrote, "Guilt make a man feel fake when he smile/ Love get confused in the mind of a child/ 'Cause love wouldn't lie like I lie and it's wild/ I wanna have my cake and another cake too/ Even if the baker don't bake like you/ Even when the flavor don't taste like you." That verse truly defines the way a lot of men think when it comes to women. Men are willing to lie and cheat just so they can continue to have sexual encounters with other women. Just to have the ability to experience something different. To taste something different!

A man who exemplifies self-control and discipline when it comes to sexual temptation chooses not to self-destruct. It simply goes back to the question "What's more important, what you want now?" or "What do you want the most?" Unfortunately, most guys lose what they want most for what they wanted at the moment. There's a price that we all pay as humans when we choose to make a choice that wasn't in our best interest, at the moment.

I know there are a lot of beautiful women in the world. Every woman comes in different shapes, sizes, personality, and qualities. There are so many women to choose from, I can truly understand how it could make a man go crazy. I believe women have more self-control than men when it comes to the opposite sex. Men are visual beings and women are emotional beings. We can fall in love with a man without sex being involved while a man can sleep with multiple women without any feelings or emotional connections. As women, we have to find some logical way to understand how men think when it comes to women. Once we understand enough of how they think and operate, then we can make better decisions and choose differently, physically, mentally and emotionally, when we decide to date.

You can't fault men for liking what they see, but we can fault them when they try to pursue what they see, knowing they aren't available to do so. When men and women finally mature, they realize that looks and sex aren't everything. As individuals, we have so much to offer that's greater than sex or appearances. Chemistry is very important because it's how someone makes you feel about yourself in their presence. Sex is supposed to be a bonus; it does not make up the foundation of a relationship or marriage. Personality and character are the qualities that we should be going after. Most women seek for equality in a relationship.

When a man reaches a point in his life where beauty and sex don't drive him to only focus on his sexual appetite, that's when he can really focus on finding a woman that meets his internal desires. How can someone touch you so deeply, stimulate your mind, challenge you to grow, and make you want to become a better version of yourself? Until a man finds someone who can fulfill those needs, pretty faces and big butts will be the only objects that get his attention. Unfortunately, I can't say that all men reach this point of maturity. Whenever I converse with women who are older than me, they always say, "Older men aren't any better. How can you teach an old dog new tricks?" You can't!

So where does that leave us, Ladies? I encourage you to continue to date and be open to meeting new people. But also, you must learn to date smart while you wait until a man comes along who will love you as you deserve. Stop giving so much of yourself away that you don't need to give in the beginning of a relationship. Keep control over yourself and your emotions. Know your worth and be patient. Patience will keep you from making poor decisions that will set you back in life. The game don't change, Ladies. But men can only do what you allow them to do.

We are only fearful of dating when we continuously make the same poor decisions over and over again in that vicious cycle. As women we have to start holding ourselves accountable for our poor choices. Men are going to be men, there's no changing that fact. But you always have control over yourself and the choices you make. A man is always going to try his hand, but his hand should never be full of you until he shows you that he is good enough and strong enough to hold you. Some men are really looking for wives but there are others who are just looking for a good time and some action.

If you're waiting for Mr. Right, sex while dating will always be your biggest downfall. It's the fastest way to commit emotional suicide, so don't do it to yourself. Sex will be the least of the concerns for a man who wants to get to know you and is really interested in courting you and pursuing you. A wise man knows when he does his part and gives his woman what she needs, everything he wants and more will soon follow. A king knows how to treat a queen and queen knows how to treat a king because in the end, they both will win together.

I recently met a guy at a store. It was late, but I stopped to get some Gatorade after work. The guy was in line in front of me and made a joke about me carrying so many Gatorades in my hand. I laughed as I was leaving and he asked me for my number. I normally don't give out my number because I'm at a place in my life where I'm extremely busy and my time is very limited. At the time, I just wanted to focus on publishing my book; dating wasn't a priority. I ended up giving him my number anyway. He was funny and made me laugh so I just ended up giving to him.

He first attempted to ask me out after ten o'clock at night. That was a complete turn-off for me right there. I don't think it's appropriate for a man to ask a woman out during those late hours. On another day, he asked me out again at 11:30 pm and wanted to hang out. I was done. It was clear that he honestly thought asking a woman out so late at night was okay. Based off my standards and what I expected, it wasn't okay for me. He ended up calling me 'damaged goods' after I refused to go. I'm not sure how sticking to my standards makes me "damaged goods" but it didn't matter.

Ladies, you have to know who you are and what you stand for. If I didn't know who I was I could have taken his insult to heart but I didn't. There are levels to dating, and there should always be boundaries. No woman should ever go out with someone she doesn't know that late at night for the first time. I'm not going to say he was just looking for some action but that time of night was just inappropriate to me. It's important to have expectations when you date and if a man doesn't meet your expectations from the beginning, there's no need to proceed. If you don't stand for something, you will fall for anything. Period.

Ladies, please continue to date, I encourage you to date but just date smart. It's great to feel strong and independent but we must remember to remain humble. The same way you are a valuable asset to a man, you should understand that the right man will also be a valuable asset to you. A man that plans to be around for a long time won't rush you into sex. A man who has no intention of being around for a while will get tired of waiting and leave anyway. So, let the bad men wean themselves out; they will be doing you a big favor. The game don't change ladies, but just because the game may be presented to you doesn't mean you have to entertain it! Instead, you can be the Game Changer!

What makes you a Game Changer? A Game Changer is a woman who makes her own rules, and stands firm in what she believes. She lays out guidelines and has standards that MUST be met! She is a woman who understands that sometimes you have to teach people how you should be treated. It's normal for most men to play games and most of the time women just fall in line and play games right along with them. Game Changers don't play games; we know who we are and we know what we want. We don't have time to play games! Game Changers are willing to keep moving rather than staying around, trying to make something out of nothing. Game Changers Don't Play the Game, We Change the Game!!!

Take this time to reflect and ask yourself,

- Am I operating in the same manner, choosing the same type of man, and making the same poor decisions when it comes to dating and relationships?

- Do I repeat the same actions while expecting different results?

- What can I start doing differently? How can I start guarding my heart with all diligence?

Ladies, don't Play the Game, Change the Game!

Remember, how you choose to treat yourself will always be the Standard of how you'll allow others to treat you.

Petty Emotions

Never give someone that much power over you where they control how you choose to react based off their actions.

— Jenise McNair

Petty Emotions: when you allow your feelings to cause you to be unstable and unreasonable.

Ladies, it is well known that we can be very emotional at times, emotional to the point where we let our feelings cloud our judgment. How can we handle our emotions as women and still make the best decisions we possibly can, especially for our children? Dealing with the failure of a relationship in the midst of bringing a child into this world is very hard, especially when the failure of the relationship is due to a heartbreak or the relationship just isn't working out in your favor.

One thing we have to learn as women is that we all have the right to change our minds. Of course, not being with the father of your child was never a possibility in your mind, but once you are no longer together, that reality is something you have to learn how to deal with. Sometimes in a relationship, a man starts out wanting one feature and then later on, he realizes he wants something else. The same holds true for women.

I often hear of women who use their kids as a way to hurt the father or to make his life miserable. Most of the time the child resides with the mother so, of course, some women use custody to their advantage as a way of controlling the situation. Perhaps you were not the one who wanted the relationship to end; the breakup may have been the father's decision. I know you might be hurting, Ladies, but you shouldn't use your child as a way to get back at the father. Telling him he can't see his child, making him come over to spend time but refusing to let him take the child with him, or requiring him to pay child support when he's doing his part, just isn't the right way to deal with your emotions. Anger and frustration will cause you to take a reactive approach versus a proactive approach because you allow your emotions to take control.

I know it's hard but as mothers, we have to make the best decisions for our children, despite how we may feel about their father. Doing the right thing is based off of a sense of fairness and the idea of how you would want someone to treat you. A man who has a child with you, unfortunately, isn't obligated to be with you. But being separated from you doesn't make him any less of a father either. As long as he hasn't put the child in harm's way, he should be able to continue to be there for his child, regardless of the status of your relationship with him. We have to do what's right, no matter how wrong he may have treated you and whether or not he wants to be in a relationship anymore. Being a single mother of three myself, I hate when my male friends tell me how the mother of their children made them pay child support, even though they are active fathers who are always there for their children. Their exes wanted them to pay, not because they weren't active fathers, but because they didn't want a relationship anymore.

Ladies, you have to understand that you can't force anyone to be with you and you shouldn't want to pressure a man to be with you. If he decides that he no longer wants to be in the relationship, then so be it. Let him step out of the relationship but still allow him to be the father he needs to be for his children. Being disagreeable, keeping him away from his children, acting difficult, and making him pay child support are choices that are only going to hurt you and your child in the long run. Why prevent him from taking care of his responsibility and doing his part because you're upset?

Child support only needs to be involved when the two parents cannot come to an agreement or the father chooses not to do his part financially. Child support shouldn't be the first solution. If anything, hold him accountable to do his part and embrace the fact that this man wants to be in his child's life. There are too many men who bring children into this world and make a choice to not be a part of their lives. So why do you want your child to go through something they don't even have to experience because you let your emotions get the best of you? How fair is that to either the father or to your child? Keeping him away from his child or making him pay child support isn't going to make him want you back. Instead, you're making him realize that walking away from the relationship was actually the best decision he could make.

We have to get to a point where we don't make permanent decisions based off temporary circumstances. Don't make a decision for the moment that is going to affect you forever. If you are a good woman but he still chose to end the relationship, take your time to heal. You are entitled to have your moments but you still need to make choices in the healthiest way you can, not through impulsive emotional decisions that will be detrimental to your children. When God closes one door, He always opens another door for us. Some things we have control over and some things we just don't have any control over. Being emotional isn't going to change a situation you don't have any power over.

When we are hurting, we don't want to look at our circumstances in a positive way but we really should. You have to speak positivity into your life. When it gets too hard for you to do so, that's when prayer comes into play. When the relationship didn't work out with my daughters' father, it sucked because I already had a son with someone else. I kept thinking, "Darn it, I have to start all over again but now with three kids!" Because I grew up in a two-parent household, not being able to give that to my children was one of the hardest realities I had to accept. But I also recognized that a two-parent household doesn't mean anything if that home is dysfunctional and the parents are miserable together. Believe it or not, children know when something is wrong; they know when their parents are unhappy. Once we become parents, our lives are really not our own and we have to make decisions that will always be in the best interest of our children. You and the father have the right to be happy even if that means him moving on and being with another woman. If one of you wants the relationship to end, for whatever reason, then you have to take the relationship for what it's worth and allow yourself to keep moving forward. I know it can be painful to see your ex move on with another woman and become everything to her that he wasn't for you. But we must understand some people just aren't the right match for one another. Or it may be at a point when a man is ready to change and a woman came along at the right time.

Don't defame your own character by trying to make the father's life miserable because you still love him and want

135

to be with him. You never know what the future holds. Maybe the two of you need a break in order to grow or maybe God has someone else in mind for you who will come along later. Stay strong and be the best mother and woman you can possibly be. At the end of the day, what's meant for you will be for you. If the father doesn't do his part and does not help his children in any way, then of course you have to take action as a mother and do what is in the best interest of your child. Which means if child support is your only option left, then so be it.

When it came to the fathers of my children, I think I was fair. I didn't ask my son's father to pay child support at first because he needed to get himself together. He had one more year left of college and I wanted him to finish, so I took care of our son. Two years later, while he was supposed to be getting himself together, he dropped out of college and ended up having another baby. At that point, I had no choice but to make sure my son had what he needed to be taken care of. Even though the father was required to pay child support, it was only for $40 every two weeks. But he wouldn't even pay that consistently.

My daughters' father also pays court-ordered child support because he used my need for his portion as a way of control. When I called for money, he said things like, "Stop stalking me. Get off my dick!" He cursed at me in every way just because he knew he had something I needed. I wasn't in a financial position to take care of our girls alone. There were times when he went months without giving me anything. If he was in a financial bind at the time, he wouldn't even communicate that to me or try to work out a deal with me. Giving me money for our daughters wasn't a top priority for him. My daughters' father later admitted that he was reactive instead of proactive at the time. He allowed his emotions to get in the way of doing what he was supposed to do. When we weren't getting along, I opened up a bank account at his bank and asked him to choose a date to make a deposit into the account every month. But he never followed through and he always dropped off the money instead; he just never wanted to cooperate during that time.

My back was up against the wall and I had to do what I needed to do, but child support was never my first solution. I thought we could be two grown adults and figure out how to care for our daughters but that was never the case for us. As a matter of fact, I only took him to court for child support because he would only give me money when he felt like giving it. I got tired of being called out by my name and arguing about when I was going to get financial help and how much I was going to get. I asked for eight hundred but he only wanted to give six hundred. Everything had to be on his terms and that's exactly how he operated in our relationship. I finally had enough. Because he was still calling me degrading names and made me jump through hoops I didn't have to, I decided to get the courts involved. That meant I wouldn't have to contact him about money and the court decided what amount was fair. But even with child support in motion, we ended up trying to make our relationship work again. You know, that same vicious cycle. That man could do anything to me and for some reason I was still willing to take him back, hoping that the potential I saw in him would take effect. He proposed to me on November 3, 2013, and I said, yes.

We had another court date for child support the very next day. I got up and got dressed. As we walked outside to get in the car, he asked me, "Are you still going through with the child support or are you going to drop the case?" I looked straight at him and said, "Based off our track record, we might be unengaged tomorrow. I can't trust that we are good until we get married." I explained to him that even though we were engaged I still had to make sure the girls were good. I couldn't trust that he wouldn't get mad at me again and stop helping. So, I told him, "While we are engaged, whatever they take out of your check for child support, I will give it right back to you." I guess what I said made sense because he wasn't mad at me and we proceeded with the case for child support. Well, Ladies, I'm glad I had the sense to keep the child support case open because by mid-December I broke off our engagement.

Being a mother, I realized that if I had to choose, I would rather have a father who was present daily but didn't have enough money to help financially than a father who was not present but paid child support. You can't pay for time and the time a father spends with his child is very valuable. I'm sure there are mothers who feel differently and wish that fathers would help out more financially. But for me, the thought of having someone else helping with homework, or giving the kids baths before I came home, or even allowing me to have a weekend to myself sounds amazing. These types of tasks are the kind of "child support" I prefer and wish the courts would order fathers to be involved in the lives of their children.

Visitation isn't mandatory like paying child support. A father who doesn't pay child support gets locked up but if he doesn't keep to his visitation schedule, the courts don't mandate that. In life, we are told to pick and choose our poison but unfortunately, as mothers, we don't get to choose. It's okay if you made mistakes and acted emotionally unstable, making decisions that were based off how you felt at the moment and not what was best for your child. We have plenty of chances to work on ourselves and make things right. You aren't the only woman who made poor decisions and tried to hurt the father of your child because you were mad and wounded inside. We all fall short sometimes, but the good news is that you have the ability to hold yourself accountable and make your situation as a co-parent right.

I've learned that a man can treat a woman terribly but somehow still be a great father. You can't hold how he treated you against him. What matters at this moment is how he chooses to treat his children. You may even find yourself saying, "He was a terrible boyfriend/ fiancé/ husband but he's a great father, I've got to give that to him." Remember, being a parent is about learning as you go, so if he wants to pick up his child and take the child back to his house, you can't worry about whether or not he will know what to do with a baby. Hell, I didn't know what to do with my first child either but I had to learn. You have to give fathers the opportunity to learn as well.

You can't micromanage him as a father, telling him he can only come over and spend time at your house, or telling him the kids always have to be with you for every holiday. As long as a father wants to be around and be a part of his child's life, then do whatever you have to do in order to co-parent with him in the healthiest and most effective way possible. Put your feelings to the side and do what's right, no matter how angry or upset you are with the father. Remember, who he is as a father has nothing to do with

139

what type of man he was to you. They are two totally different elements of who he is.

Even though my situation was different, trying to get a hold of my emotions was something that I had to learn, as well. I walked away from my daughters' father and even though I left, I still had so much anger built up inside of me because of how he treated me when we were together. I finally realized that how he treated me had nothing to do with my daughters or his ability to act like a father. Of course, he tried to hurt me by not coming to get the girls, saying that the girls weren't his, and withholding money from them. I had to learn how to function without allowing him to make me emotionally distraught. There was a time when he had his moment, after I gave the engagement ring back, and did whatever he wanted to do.

It was a hard reality to accept that he was going to continue to operate however he wanted to. I couldn't control his anger or disrespectfulness toward me, so I had to work on myself and try to change the areas I needed to work on. I got to the point where I stopped entertaining his foolishness and I refused to react to his impulsive behavior. I realized he did a lot of things just to get a reaction out of me, so I chose to stop reacting.

In the same way women can be emotional, men can be even more emotional. They just handle their problems differently. Instead of trying to find a solution to a problem, they prefer to find a solution that will feed their pride and make them feel better. Calling me out by my name made him feel better. Belittling me made him feel better. Telling himself that I was the problem made him feel better. Over time, I realized he was a Narcissist and there was no way to reason with him. In his mind it was 'his way or no way.' Period. I had to grow as a woman and understand that I couldn't allow my ex to dictate my mood based off his actions. I couldn't continue to put my life in jeopardy by arguing with him, knowing I had a heart condition. I got to a point where I stopped arguing with him about spending more time with the girls. There were times he saw the girls only once every three weeks because working was his excuse. I realized you can't make a grown person do something they don't want to do.

I invited him to birthday parties but he asked me, "Why? We aren't together, so why am I going to show up acting and faking like we are together and we're not?" I reminded him that the party was not about us, it was for our daughters. And at the end of the day, they wanted their dad at their party. He decided that we would have separate parties and I agreed to that decision. What's funny is as the years went by, he got upset that I didn't invite him to the girls' birthday parties! Did he forget that he didn't want to come to the parties? I seemed like the bad guy because I just accepted what he wanted and stopped asking him to come.

One lesson you will learn is that no matter what, you will always have to co-exist with your child's father if they take an active role. The best choice to make is to always keep your children in mind and do what's best for them. For years, I prayed and asked God to make the conditions better between the two of us for the sake of our daughters. God told me to work on myself and He would take care of him. I started to grow as a woman and a person and after a while, I learned how to pick and choose my battles with him. I learned how to put our relationship behind me and leave it in the past. I was able to grow by finally accepting that things aren't always going to play out the way you would like and that's okay. There's truly beauty beyond our pain.

Despite the pain he caused me throughout the years; we still created two of the most beautiful little girls in the world together. Fighting for our relationship to work only encouraged me to fight for my own inner happiness and peace. I went above and beyond for myself and took the time out to really learn who Jenise was. He broke me down but I learned how to build a better version of me. The hardship that our relationship caused me truly made me a better and wiser woman.

Our relationship didn't work out but at the end of the day, he was still the father of my daughters and I still had to deal with him, whether I wanted to or not. I left before my daughters were old enough to know what was taking place between their father and I but as they got older, they asked why we lived separately. Why did they have to have two homes? How come we weren't a family? Why didn't I talk to their daddy? I sent a video of my oldest daughter asking these questions and his response was, "You made her say that stuff." The video was three minutes long; what five-year old could remember to say all that? But again, his reality was his perception, she spoke from the heart but he wanted to believe I made her say those things.

I was willing to try to include him for the sake of our daughters. I asked to meet at a park to do something as a family but he didn't want to. He wasn't in the space I was in, which made me mad at first, but I had to remember I couldn't change anyone but myself. I had to leave what I couldn't change to God. At one point, my sister acted as the mediator between the two of us. Anytime we needed to communicate with each other she was on the text message thread. Yes, two grown adults needed another grown person on our text thread because we just couldn't get along. The situation started to get better to the point where we joked with each other. My sister said to me, "Well, look at God. Y'all over there cracking jokes." Over time, our relationship as co-parents improved greatly although it still could be better.

I promise you, prayer really works. He finally became a very supportive co-parent. Instead of being enemies, we are really learning how to be a team. Two is always better than one, especially when it comes down to raising your children. I am quick to tell you that nothing happens overnight; everything in life is truly a process. Right now, we are doing well at caring for our daughters; yet we are still a work in progress. I am praying that one day we are going to be *great* co-parents.

When our relationship was going completely wrong, and he got upset with me and disrespected me by calling me out by name, I chose to label items as what I wished for them to be. For years, I listed his name in my phone as, "The Girls' Great Father." No matter how upset I was at him or how much I felt like I hated him, I kept his name in my phone like that. Dealing with him caused me to experience so much hurt and pain, I had to create a positive place within myself where I could feed my spirit. Most importantly, I had to learn to forgive him. No matter what the situation looked like at the moment, I kept telling myself, things are going to get better, just keep working on you, and leave what you can't change to God.

My daughters' father used to get upset that I always contacted other people first instead of making him the first option for taking care of our girls. We didn't get along so instead of starting an argument, I always asked my sister or my dad to help me out. But my thought process at the time had a lot to do with my petty emotions. I allowed for my emotions to believe that if I asked him to do something, he would just say, "No!"

Then one day, my sister said, "Jenise, you need to start making him the first option when it comes to the girls." She reminded me that he needed to be more involved and help out since he is their father. After two weeks of her encouragement to involve him more, I told myself, "Jenise, put your pride to the side and start asking him for help. If he says no, then keep moving and come up with another plan."

Well, when I started asking, he began to help out more. He took the girls to the dentist or doctor and picked them up on days I had to work late. He truly became a team player and it was great having him for support. Aunties, uncles, and even grandparents are great for helping raise a child but there's nothing like a child with two parents involved.

Emotions can cause us to be stubborn and prideful but as you grow as a person, you start to realize being a parent really isn't about you, it's about the children. We have to learn how to deal with our emotions in the healthiest way by holding ourselves accountable. Now, I'm not going to put all the blame on women and say we are the only ones being petty when it comes to our emotions or making wise decisions for our kids because, clearly, we aren't. But because I am a woman, I wanted to address the situation from a woman's perspective.

Despite any personal feelings that you may have toward the father of your kids, you still owe it to your children to be the best mother you can possibly be. You aren't being the best mother you can be if you choose to be petty and keep the kids away from their father or put him on child support just because he no longer wants to be in a relationship. That control is just not fair to your children, so you have to do better in that area. You overcome your pettiness by choosing your child's best interest first. You overcome your petty emotions by not making everything about you or how you feel. Whenever you find yourself on the verge of being petty, I want you to start thinking about your child and ask yourself if the decision you are about to make will hurt them or help them. We cannot change anything about ourselves without effort. You overcome the ties between your emotions as a woman and your responsibility as a mother by always choosing to put your child first. Your pettiness is not going to stop overnight but every day is a new day to make an effort and try for your child's sake.

The next area I want to address that often causes us to be emotional, is a part that people on the outside don't see. This situation occurs when the father plays games with your heart, sending you mixed signals. You aren't in a relationship, but when he comes to see the children, you somehow find yourself sitting on his lap, if you know what I mean. Ladies, listen to me when I tell you, making a choice to have sex with the father of your children when you aren't together is one of the biggest mistakes you can possibly make. You instantly commit emotional suicide.

145

You will forever be petty if you allow yourself to be in a situation of uncertainty, confusion, and hopefulness.

The day I decided that I was done with my ex, I was really done, even after being with him for five years. To this day the father of my daughters and I have never crossed those lines again; we've never come remotely close to being physically involved. If you are not together but you still decide to have to have sex with him, then he doesn't owe you anything. Just because he is the father of your child doesn't mean you owe him anything either. You are not obligated to continue to sleep with him just because you had his baby. Now if you have an understanding that sex is just what it is, then so be it. But make sure you really can handle what comes along with casual sex.

Unfortunately, that is usually not the case when you still sleep with your child's father. He might tell you that you two are going to get back together, he still loves you, and all that good stuff. Then, you find out he's dealing with another woman. That's when you try to make his life a living hell because he's clearly playing with your emotions. But you allowed him to. You can't get mad at him because a man can only do what we allow. If you give him permission to come over and have sex whenever he wants with no commitment to you, then you can't be mad at anyone but yourself when the situation gets complicated. And if you just can't control yourself when he comes over, then you need to put other arrangements in place that will be best for you, such as meeting him outside the house instead of letting him inside.

When my girls were younger and their father picked them up, he was still very, very attractive. I felt so mad because I

146

couldn't stand him personally so I hated the fact I was still attracted to him. I didn't want to be attracted to him physically because I disliked him so much for everything that he put me through. Again, we have to learn how to walk in our truth and accept the things that have taken place in our life that we can't change. Just because we weren't together didn't mean he stopped being attractive, yet he just wasn't the man for me. One year, I went to the girl's awards ceremony and he walked in. I didn't realize it was him at first, so I said to myself, "Ooooh! Whose Daddy is that?" As he got closer, I realized it was him and said, "Oh, that's just my baby daddy."

I had to get the place where I accepted that he was just an attractive man. Despite how he treated me, my dislike for him wasn't going to change his looks. If you struggle with still wanting the father of your kids in a sexual way, find a neutral place to let him pick up the children so there is no opportunity to get physically involved. I get it, you may still love him and hope there's a chance for you to be a happy family. But don't sleep with him based off of a potential future that unfortunately, may never happen. Yes, you are the mother of his child but you don't owe him anything other than trying to be a great co-parent with him. Do yourself a favor and keep sex out of the equation because it will do more damage than good.

The only time I slept with the father of my daughters was when I thought we were working on getting back together, or when I knew deep down inside, I was hoping he would change and things would get better. Whenever I broke up with him, I always considered the time apart as a temporary break because I still operated as if we were together, whether he did or not. Once I made a choice to be completely done, having sex with him was never a thought, despite his attractiveness. His attractiveness didn't outweigh his inability to love me and respect me the way I deserved to be treated.

When a woman is done emotionally and mentally with a man and a relationship that doesn't bring her happiness, making choices that interfere with her plan to move on just isn't an option for her. Most women still end up in messy situations because they are still in love or they hold on to the potential of what their relationship together could be. You can't avoid being in messy situations until you are truly honest with yourself about where you are in life and the expectations that you set for yourself. I value myself and I believe that I am a good woman, so why would I even give my ex the satisfaction of using my body whenever he wanted? There's no way!

You have to get a point where you choose to put yourself first and never settle for anything less than what you deserve. You'll get to this point when you start to love yourself more than anyone or anything. When you truly love yourself first, you will be more conscious of the decisions you make and will start making wiser choices that are in your best interest.

If the father was the reason why you ended the relationship, whether he wanted out of it or he cheated and did you wrong, why in the world would you ever consider letting him even touch you again? He wanted to walk away to 'find himself' but still wants to have sex with you without any commitment to you? That deal should never happen. Listen, Queens, you are worth so much more than being used by a man and you deserve what God has for you.

Believe me, that mess isn't His will. End this vicious cycle, focus on you, and be the best mother you can be for your children.

Allowing your emotions to cause you to be petty isn't what is best for your children. The first step to change is accepting and admitting that change is necessary in that area. Walking in your truth and accepting that the relationship is over, means that the children you two share should be the only focus. Starting there would make a world of a difference. I understood that I couldn't and wouldn't reach my full potential in life by being petty just because I was unable to control my emotions.

You deserve to have God's best for your life so you can't allow someone to have that much control over your reactions and feelings. The emotional decisions that you choose to make, all because you are feeling petty, aren't worth your child's happiness. As parents, we are often so caught up in our emotions and so focused on our own feelings, that we don't take the time out to consider our children's feelings. We make everything about us and not enough about the child. Being emotional and petty only affects the child in the long run. When you keep the father from his child, you only hurt your child. When a father disrespects the mother in front of the child, calling her degrading names and belittling her, the child is the one who is affected.

When we both focus on doing all that we can to hurt one another, we fail to realize that we are only working together to destroy our children's happiness. Our children and their happiness should be worth the choice to become the bigger person, the choice to compromise, the choice to deny your own emotions, and the choice to always make an effort to do what's right for them. The day we decided to have children was the day we chose to always put our children before ourselves. Even though not getting along with the other parent of your child can be very challenging, you must come to understand, it's not about you or what you want anymore.

At the end of the day, it's about what our children want and what's best for them. Our children watch us, even when we think they aren't paying attention. It's never too late to change for the better, especially if your child's happiness depends on it. I know this will be a very hard adjustment to make but it's a change that's necessary. You owe it to yourself and your children to try to be the best woman and mother you can be.

Remember, how you choose to treat yourself will always be the Standard of how you'll allow others to treat you.

Growing Pains

The key to becoming the woman you've always wanted to be, is still believing you will become that woman even in the midst of mistakes, obstacles, and storms.

— Jenise McNair

From the time we were born to our present day, growth is just something that is a big part of life. From little girls, to pre-teens, to teenagers, to young women, and finally as grown women, we will encounter a lot of growing pains. What are growing pains? My personal definition is that growing pains are personal experiences that we encounter in life that caused us hurt but also allowed us to develop as individuals so that we can make better decisions in the future.

Are you able to recognize when you go through growing pains? That ability really depends on where you are in life and how much you have already grown as a woman. Have you ever heard the saying, "Sometimes in life, your situation will keep repeating itself until you've learned your lesson or you have grown from it?" I believe there's a lot of truth to that statement, especially when we keep finding ourselves in the same, compromising situations when it comes to the men we choose. That same vicious cycle that causes us to continuously make the same choice, ending up in the same place, operating in the same manner, that gives us the same result, every single time.

It was really tough for me to distinguish what I needed to do differently when it came to choosing a man. I continuously dated men based on their looks and their potential and tried to do all that I could to make them better. I kept consciously dating men who hadn't dealt with their past trauma and I chose to try to love them past their pain. I kept thinking that I had the power to fix and change them for the better. Since I continued to make those same decisions, I kept getting the same results, foolishly thinking one day my way would work. Because I was not able to recognize what I needed to change, I continued to allow myself to be hurt over and over.

One of the biggest mistakes that I made was thinking I could change and love men past their pain. I always attracted men that suffered internally, struggled with how to love, or just did not know their own worth. I chose to carry their burdens and that was just detrimental to them and to me. Sometimes we need to just to be still and sit in our own pain. This will allow you to reflect on the hurt, asking yourself, "Is this pain something I want to continue to endure? What choices did I make that put me in this position?"

If you can't understand how you ended up in your current circumstance, then that means you're mostly likely going to end up there again. Sitting in your pain helps you to reflect and evaluate your circumstances. Ask yourself, "Why do I feel this way? What was the red flag that I chose to overlook?" Red flags always exist in the beginning yet when we want something so badly, we are willing to overlook the warnings that we shouldn't. Sitting in your pain will allow you to reflect and really think about what signs you ignored that made you later endure unnecessary pain. We have to be able to recognize how we got in the predicament that we are in so we won't allow ourselves to end up there again.

Growing pains in life aren't a negative aspect, they help you to build character and definitely cause you to become wiser. You hear the saying all the time, "Some people just have to learn the hard way!" I was that person, always wanting to do things my way and thinking I could help everybody. I continued making the same choices and caused myself unnecessary pain as well. Those pains I endured caused me to grow, to become wiser, and to make better choices. Who wants to keep making the same choices that inflict unintentional pain on themselves? Life experiences cause each and every one of us to grow. Some people may learn more slowly than others but growth still takes place in the process.

The guy who I had a relationship with after my daughters' father, told me early while dating that he had commitment issues, yet I continued to allow myself to spend time with him. He mentioned to me that when things were going well and seemed too good to be true, he usually acted out or made up an excuse to sabotage his relationships with every woman he dated. But, he was tall and handsome, with a muscular physique, a nice smile, a very personable personality and he always smelled so good. Before I met him, he spent a good portion of his life in the streets as well, operating with that same street mentality. He was an Alpha male; he never wanted me to pay for anything and always made me feel safe and secure. Well, we all know the more time you spend with someone, the more you grow attached to them.

Every day that we spent together was another day that I grew closer to him and wanted to know more about him. We had great chemistry, we laughed, we smiled, and we were able to be open with one another. When making a decision on whether or not he was someone that I could see myself with, I allowed my emotions to overlook the truth. The truth was, no matter how much joy he brought to my life, I continued to ignore the fact that he told me he struggled with commitment. I thought our relationship would be different. I believed that deep down, he wanted to actually face his fears of commitment.

Can you imagine putting everything into a relationship, holding absolutely nothing back, then out of the blue your man runs away from the relationship, just when you thought everything was going well. I felt DEVASTATED! He left with nothing more than an, "It's not you, it's me!" "Yes, you're right," I said to myself, "It is you because you're an idiot for walking away from a good woman." He wasn't really an idiot; he was a good man to my children and me which is why the breakup hurt as much as it did.

Some guys are truly intimidated by a good woman. Being with a good woman can cause a man to want to put his best foot forward and become a better version of himself. Then there are other men who are at a point in their lives when they just don't want to have to live up to a certain expectation at the moment. He told me that he wasn't where he needed to be in life financially to be with a woman who had three kids. During my relationship with my daughters' father, I received jewelry, expensive gifts, or whatever I asked for. Giving me money was never an issue for him but giving me respect was.

But then, I found myself in another relationship where respect and happiness were present but not having enough money was an issue. I tried to explain to him that I didn't care if he had a lot of money; I only cared about how happy he made my children and me. He was a hard worker who always had more than one job. My happiness was worth so much more than what money could ever buy. Our love was simple yet *Amazing!* He expressed to me that I gave him the very best times of his life yet he still made a decision to walk away.

At the time that our ways parted, of course I was hurt. I couldn't understand his logic. But I stepped away from my own feelings and tried to place myself in his shoes. He recognized that I was a good woman who raised three children and worked three jobs. I never put the responsibility on him to take care of my children, but it was still an obligation he felt like he wanted to do as my man. Of course he wasn't trying to replace my children's fathers but he still wanted to be in a financial position to be there if help was ever needed. He wasn't happy with his finances, so meeting an incredible woman with a built-in family was just pressure he wasn't ready for.

Even though he chose to walk away and I respected his decision, he still couldn't leave me alone. Every month or so he drove past my house or contacted me in some way, giving me mixed signals. I allowed this attention to go on for years. He told me how he made a mistake and that he should never have walked away but he needed to get himself together. He was so indecisive; he just didn't know what he wanted. It felt like he didn't want to do what it took to be with me, even though he had a very hard time living without me. His character was far more valuable and worthy than any amount of money he could ever make. But that was the problem; he didn't believe that fact and I knew I couldn't be with a man who didn't know his own worth. As painful as it was, I had to accept the fact that he needed to find his own healing and truth to walk in first. Our own personal truth will get in the way of our future if we don't learn how to deal with it.

Every situation in life has a cause and effect. Sometimes you just have to ask yourself, "What should I have done differently? What were the red flags that I chose to overlook?" He told me in the very beginning he had commitment issues and he also mentioned he found ways to sabotage his relationships when they seemed to be going well. Why did I choose to ignore his truth? Why did I think he would handle our relationship differently? He did everything in our relationship that he said he normally did. He sabotaged it and then ran. I chose to overlook the red flags because I didn't want to accept his truth but he went into the relationship and led me to believe he could do things differently. We both chose to overlook the inevitable.

Sometimes you look back at the beginning of your circumstance and see the pieces that are wrong and all you can do is shake your head. In both of my adulthood relationships, there was a moment that each man looked me in the eyes and said he felt that I was an angel that was sent to him. But they both said it in a way as if they believed my purpose was to save them; I was their light! Everything that women decide to overlook in the very beginning is the same reason why we are hurt in the end. This goes back to what I mentioned earlier, our situation will keep repeating itself until you've learned your lesson or you have grown from it. How many times are we going to inflict pain on ourselves because we keep making the same poor choices? I believe there is purpose for the pain that we endure.

What is the reason for growing pains? These pains we encounter cause us to grow into better and wiser people. Growing pains don't feel good at the time; I won't lie to you and tell you that they do. But the wisdom that you gain from the pain makes it all worthwhile. I'm sorry to say this, but growing pains are never ending, yet they continue to cause us to develop in every aspect of our lives. Growing pains allowed me to dig deeper into who I was as a woman, helping me to find the greater good within myself.

When I lost my mother at the age of 23, the pain that I felt seemed unbearable. Grieving is a type of growing pain. I didn't think I was strong enough to endure losing either one of my parents. Yet, the pain that I felt deep within pushed me to become a better version of myself. Growing up, I used to say, "If anything ever happened to my parents, I don't know if I would be strong enough to push on without them." Now, here I am, learning to push on every day without my mother. Pain can drive you or pain can drain you.

There's pain that we create for ourselves based on our own decisions and then there's pain that we have no control over. No matter how much you've been hurt or how much pain you've endured, I need you to know, you can and you will overcome it. Sometimes, you hit rock bottom and the top just seems so far away. But every day is a step that gets you closer to the goals you set out to achieve, as long as you don't give up. There was a time when I was struggling, I expected someone close to me to be there for me but they weren't. That betrayal crushed my heart because I had always been there for them. But God allowed that disappointment to show me that I didn't need anybody but Him. God solely wanted me to Trust Him.

From every life experience that caused me pain, I learned to be positive, even in the midst of the storms. The pain I encountered in my life made me have a different perspective towards each day and how I choose to deal with my circumstances. One point we have to realize, not just as women but as people, is that, no matter what, we have control over how we choose to react to our situation. Even when pain is involved, we have the power and the inner strength to still make sound decisions.

There are so many levels and types of pain that we may encounter. Physical and emotional pain affects every individual in different ways. I honestly believe that the level of pain that you encounter can either break you down or build you up. Determining which direction that you take solely depends on what you want for yourself. Most people who encounter growing pains lack the understanding of why they go through situations that cause them pain. Certain painful circumstances can seem unbearable, making someone question, "Do I really want to be here anymore? Is there anyone in my life that truly loves me?" After losing my mom, I felt that pain constantly, deep within my soul, but over time, I had to learn how to deal with that heartache. It was that type of pain that made me question, if I even wanted to be alive without her. If it wasn't for my son, I'm not sure where I would be today. His love kept me going. I understood that I owed it to my son to give him the best life I could possibly give him as his mother because that's what my mother did for me.

Pain causes some people to hit rock bottom, because at that moment, it's too unbearable to even function. If you get to that point, the best thing you can do for yourself is pray. You have to pray for strength and perseverance. I've learned through the years that each and every one of us has a purpose on this earth. Each and every one of us is uniquely made and we bring our individual strengths to the world. We are all special in our own way and our growing pains can lead us to that purpose. Our purpose is all the power we will ever need in life. Pain turns into Passion and your Passion directs you to your Purpose. As crazy as it sounds, there's truly beauty in your brokenness. Pain can most definitely break us down to absolutely nothing but the beauty about being broken is that you can rebuild yourself to be stronger and better than ever before.

Every chance I get, I tell my clients that they have an opportunity to restore their foundation and sense of security within themselves by making the necessary adjustments to feel safe and weather any storms they encounter in life. Understand that when you choose to build a connection, whether it's a friendship or any type of relationship, the foundation is the most important part. The foundation is what keeps everything together. When we think of a lasting friendship or relationship, it's often built off trust, loyalty, respect, honesty, love, and support. Everyone is in a hurry to move swiftly ahead and no one wants to take the time to lay a strong and secure foundation until the day everything, including ourselves, comes falling down. This destruction takes place because no one wants to be patient and trust the process.

Everywhere you look today, houses are built so quickly. The builders want to make certain deadlines so that they can sell the houses and then make money. The companies who build this way lose the integrity of their businesses in the long run. Instead of focusing on quality and making sure the foundations of these homes are strong, they care only about quantity and flipping the house quickly so they can sell it.

Integrity is also important for our relationships but most of them are compromised from the very beginning because we don't take the time to build and lay a strong foundation. As children, it wasn't our responsibility to lay a strong foundation for ourselves, we were too young to even know how. Parents must be responsible to lay a strong and secure foundation for their children. The foundation that my parents laid for me, was the reason why I was able to finally walk away from the abusive relationship I was in. I allowed myself to remain in it for a time, but I remembered who I was and where I came from because of the foundation that my parents laid for me. Somewhere in trying to make my daughters' father better, I also knew I deserved better for myself.

We have to understand that God allows us to go through growing pains just to get our attention. If you keep finding yourself in the same vicious cycle, you haven't gotten to the point where you had enough and you will keep going through those same steps until you are ready to finally move forward. Some people never get unstuck because they choose to remain stuck. We have the power and ability to change any circumstance we are in, but that change depends on what you are willing to do to remove yourself from it. Ladies, we have to start making better decisions and stop rushing into relationships with men just to be able to say we have a man. Allow your growing pains to build you up so that you will be strong enough to walk away from any situation or anyone that you know isn't right for you.

Ask yourself what keeps recurring in your life? Do you believe that situation keeps happening because God is trying to get your attention? Growing pains are meant for your growth: mentally, physically, emotionally, and most importantly, spiritually. Make a choice today to stop inflicting pain on yourself and move forward in your life, doing the things that truly bring you happiness.

Remember, how you choose to treat yourself will always be the Standard of how you'll allow others to treat you.

Women of Strength

The Strength of a Woman will Strengthen another Woman.

— Jenise McNair

It truly takes a lot of strength to be a woman today, especially a woman that your children and parents can be proud of. A woman you want to look at in the mirror and admire. The day-to-day agendas that we follow can feel overbearing, stressful, and exhausting. Yet, we have to keep ourselves together physically, mentally, and emotionally. There are days where we feel like the only progress we made is giving to others and that effort empties out every tool that's in our survival tanks. Previously, I wavered between trying to save an unhappy relationship, keeping my sanity so my kids wouldn't know how miserable I was, working all day to make something out of nothing, and then looking presentable so no one knew what was actually taking place in my life. That struggle was absolutely draining and exhausting!

I honestly felt like I emptied myself out but there was nothing left inside of me to pull from. I felt like I was living but I wasn't really alive. My body was here physically but mentally, spiritually, and emotionally I was completely lost. I was at a point where something had to give because I was on the verge of giving up. Enough was enough. I couldn't go another day living a lie and pretending like I was winning. I wanted to really know what it felt like to be in control of my own happiness and win.

I'll never forget the day I fell to my knees and I just surrendered it all to God. I cried like a baby because I was ready to stop living a lie. I was finally ready to accept all of the pain and trauma I tried to run away from. Instead of making myself believe the lies I told, I started the process of owning my truth. The day I accepted the reality of what happened to me that I didn't want to remember, I instantly became free. I allowed myself to start the process of healing by acknowledging the truth, which gave me the strength to move forward. Walking in your truth will give you all the strength you'll ever need in life. God is our first source of power that we can pull from. But without choosing to walk in truth, you'll never maximize your strength to its capacity.

I still remember so vividly the day I discovered my own strength. That day, my father called me and told me that my mother passed away. I was ready to walk out the door to go to the hospital and see her. As soon as the words left his mouth, I instantly dropped to the floor, crying and screaming uncontrollably. You never think the worst can happen to you until it does. I instantly went completely numb throughout my body. I laid on the floor feeling this way for about ten minutes. Then I told myself that I had to get it together; I had to pull from whatever strength I had left and actually drive to the hospital to see my mother. Although I wanted to lie there for as long as I could, doing absolutely nothing but crying, I knew that I couldn't.

The day I lost my mom was the day I lost myself as well. That incident was the pivotal moment in my life as an adult where I was present but I wasn't "present." I physically existed but I felt like a big part of me left with my mother. I had no ambition, no drive, and no desire to try to accomplish goals or make an effort at all. I honestly didn't care what each day forward would bring. It no longer mattered to me; nothing was worse than the feeling of losing the most important woman in my life. I was in a hopeless state of mind!

I was only twenty-three and had a three-year old. Up to that point, my mom was a super-grandma even while she was ill. Her sickness never stopped her from being the best grandmother she could possibly be to her first grandchild; a grandson who looked exactly like her. On the nights when I felt sleep-deprived and barely could focus, my mom came into my room, took my son, and kept him with her throughout the night so I could rest. My son never wanted for anything. She kissed and hugged him endlessly as if she never wanted to let him go. Like most grandmothers, she treated him like her son. My mother and my father helped deliver my son. They were always there for him, showering him with love and affection.

After the call from my dad, I made it to the hospital but I didn't know what to expect. I didn't want to act foolishly when I saw her lying in the hospital bed, knowing she was gone. I braced myself as I walked into the room. There she was so beautiful. She had this angelic smile on her face as if she had seen God himself or maybe my grandmother who passed only nine months before her. Once I saw that smile on her face, there was no way I could cry. I knew she was free; free from pain and free from sickness. At that very moment, I wanted to go wherever she had gone. I wanted to be free from the unbearable pain I felt because I didn't know how I could live without her.

You never know how strong you have to be until being strong is your only option. In the moments after my mom passed, God definitely tested my strength. While making the funeral arrangements, my sister and I helped my dad get all of the details together. When we finally saw my mother for the viewing of her body, I couldn't believe how awful her hair looked. My mother was a Diva, the type of woman who got dressed without a strand of hair out of place just to go down the street to the 7-Eleven. She was always fly and well put together. We all felt devastated when we saw her hair, knowing there was no way we could lay her to rest like that. So, I did what I had to do. I fixed my mother's hair for her funeral.

How I felt at that moment wasn't even important. I found inner strength to do what was best for my mother. So, I made a choice to do my mother's hair even though it was an emotional process. I lifted her head up and styled her hair. Her face was kind of soft, yet cold. I stared my mother in the face, fixing her bangs to fall a certain way on her forehead. And in that moment, I knew she was gone. I knew she couldn't respond to me, yet I never cried. Her hair was way more important than my pain at that moment. Although she wasn't physically there, I believe her spirit is what kept me calm. Looking at her, I could hear her voice saying, "Thank you, Baby Girl." That moment is now a memory I cherish and I'm so glad I found the strength to be there for my mother when she needed me.

My sister later commented to me, "I don't know how you just did that without falling out all over the place." But I knew that my calm response couldn't be anything other than God's strength. Can you imagine being in that moment, looking at your mother and knowing she is gone physically? Just styling her hair, like she could respond to you at some point. God's strength is truly amazing. He said He'll never leave you nor forsake you and at the moment, He was my source of strength. God is our peace, comfort, joy, and love. While styling my mother's hair I felt all of His comfort.

For her funeral, I chose to write a poem in honor of my mother to share what type of woman and mother she was. I thought about getting someone else to read the poem but I wanted to share it myself. I was worried that I would get to the middle of the poem and break down or even that I might read the first sentence and fall out. When it was my turn to speak, my siblings stood by my side as I read the poem entitled, "Phenomenal Women." I read every word correctly and pronounced every syllable clearly until the very end. After the funeral, people walked up to me saying, "I wouldn't be able to read the first sentence without breaking down, yet you read the entire poem!"

I knew in that moment, in order to honor her, I needed to be a reflection of the strength that she exemplified my whole life, especially during the last three years as she fought a terminal illness. Even when my grandmother passed away nine months earlier, my mother, despite her sickness, gathered strength and planned my grandmother's funeral as if she wasn't connected to a feeding tube. The strength she displayed during her entire illness was simply incredible. I owed it to her to display that same strength while honoring her and celebrating her life.

I wish I could say I continued in that same strength afterwards but I didn't. Losing a loved one doesn't really hit you until the whirlwind after the funeral settles down.

166

You still look for their daily phone calls, kisses, and warm hugs.

But unfortunately, I had no time to grieve after my mom's passing because I had to deal with emotional anger two weeks after my mother was buried. Her so-called 'best friend' of 40 years did the unthinkable. She started going around to my mother's siblings and close friends, telling them lies, making them think they were secrets that my mom told her in confidence. She told my mother's only sister private matters so she would perceive my mother in an unfavorable way. A best friend can say they know all of your secrets and here my mom's 'best friend' going house to house, trying to defame my mother's character! What pissed me off the most was the fact that she waited until my mother was gone and couldn't defend herself.

My mother's so-called best friend was a coward. When I found out what she tried to do, I lost my temper. Not only did I have to deal with the fact that I lost my Queen but I had to face the reality that this coward tried to defame my mother's character so soon after her passing. I had no time to be sad; I was FURIOUS! I wrote her a letter telling her how much of a coward she was for her schemes.

I am still a reflection of my parents, so never once did I curse at or threaten her in my letter. I told her exactly what I thought of her actions but I did it with self-dignity and class. My mother taught me that lesson. I spoke the truth and told her she was wrong for what she tried to do to my mother. That woman was the godmother of my older siblings and my mom was the godmother of her two children.

No one knew if she told the truth but the fact that she spread stories like that, showed me that she had no integrity or loyalty. Why would anyone even believe someone like that? Yet, she went house to house sharing secrets like she had a whole checklist.

My mother was loved by so many and that woman tried to get people to change how they felt about her. She played the part of a "'best friend' of forty years, only to find out she was my mom's number-one enemy after all! "Keep your friends close but keep your enemies closer," is a wise statement. When people show you who they are the first time, believe them. My mother always forgave her friend for her inconsiderate actions and felt bad for her. So, maybe my mom would not have been shocked by her scheming.

With all that drama going on, grieving was just too much for me to bear at the time. Instead of healing correctly and allowing myself to mourn, I did what I knew best and pretended. I proceeded to go about life, telling myself that my mom was on vacation. I never wanted to look at pictures of her and I never cried much either. I acted like losing my Queen never happened, the same story I told myself after I was molested at six-years old. To make matters even worse, the oldest son of my mom's 'best friend' was actually the person who molested me. Now you see why I chose to carry that burden for so many years? The terrible mess that secret would have caused! I never thought for one second my mom wouldn't have believed me, but I didn't want her to have to deal with the hurricane that would have taken place in her friendship.

Looking back now, I wish I would've never carried such a painful burden, trying to save a friendship that wasn't worth saving. Realizing what she tried to do to my mother's memory only made me remember what her son did to me. I thought, "Lord, take me now. I just can't deal with all this pain." The grief over both situations was just too much pain for me to bear! I kept telling myself that I had to be strong. But my definition of strong meant continuing to move forward as if nothing happened, even though I felt completely shattered on the inside.

Choosing not to grieve caused me so much more torment in the long run that forced me to deal with it anyway. I didn't want to walk in my truth because the truth was just too painful to bear. But I created even more of a mess for myself by not grieving properly at the time. It's natural to think that running away or ignoring the unbearable pain is the best decision at the time, but it's not. Refusing to face the hurt is just a way for the devil to be able to control you when you choose to run from the truth. He'll use your truth against you until you learn how to accept it and walk in it. You can't conquer what you don't confront.

It took me five years to finally convince myself to grieve and heal from the loss of my Queen. By the time I made that decision, I'd created an even bigger mess for myself. I left an abusive relationship of five years, had two more children out of wedlock, was diagnosed with a heart condition, and after twenty years, finally spoke up about being molested at six. I experienced and endured so much pain on so many levels. Some of the hurts I had no control over but I inflicted more pain on myself by making poor decisions. Finally choosing to face my past hurts was the moment when I took control back over my life. I finally decided I no longer was going to let the devil use my pain against me by making me feel hopeless and helpless.

169

Besides God's strength, facing my pain and walking in my truth is what gave me inner power to overcome my past pain and learn to fight to regain myself. We honestly cannot conquer what we don't confront. We'll never find a solution if we don't address the problem.

No matter what we go through, I believe the strength of a woman is what truly makes us incredible beings. Despite the pain I faced, I realized that I owed it to my parents, to my children, and especially to myself to learn how to walk in my truth. With God as my first source of strength, walking in my truth empowered me even more. Overcoming your trials and tribulations, one day at a time, are the moments that keep you going. Those are the moments that give you hope; those are the moments that show how you can create happiness while going through hardship. Being a woman of strength means that sometimes you have to make very hard decisions that are in your best interest, even though you want to avoid them. As women, we have to learn how to ignore the temptations that our flesh may desire and really learn how to tap into our mental strength.

Developing mental toughness will always assist you through any storm or obstacles that may come your way. Everything we accomplish starts in our minds! We become what we believe and if you feel defeated it's because you think you're already defeated. I didn't persevere and overcome all the obstacles in my life by thinking negatively. Without mental toughness, I would still be too poor to feed my kids and forty pounds overweight. I conquered every single circumstance by simply remaining positive and believing that I could overcome anything. No matter how small the victory was, the fact that I achieved a victory was good enough for me. As I started to change my thought process, I saw positive elements manifest in my life. I became more successful in my business, got a hold of my health, and ran five marathons. Once I saw what I could achieve, my mindset toward life never changed. I created that, "I can. I am. and I will." mindset.

The best thing about all of your accomplishments should be the fact that you never let hardship stop you from accomplishing them.

Nothing can ever get in the way of having God's best except you. Having God by your side and on your team already makes you a winner. You can beat ANYTHING!!!You just have to believe that He wants His best for you and apply that same mindset to every circumstance that presents itself in your life. Making sure you are healthy mentally and physically should be a priority, your number-one priority. Having God's best makes sure you are doing your part in every aspect of your life. God directs us but it's up to us to move forward in the direction He guides us. You are the captain of your ship and if the captain isn't alright, there's a strong possibility that ship and everyone on it are going to go down too.

I believe men are naturally physically stronger than women but we are hands-down, naturally stronger mentally. We endure so much, we deal with so much, and we are counted on so much by so many people. This reliance shows how we mentally prepare ourselves to delegate so much at one time. We have to mentally prepare ourselves before anything else can take place. We think of a plan and we execute it! We make it happen by all means necessary. I don't care what anyone says, women hold down the responsibilities that come with life. We know how to multitask on a level that's out of this world. Between our work demands, mom demands, girlfriend/wife demands, and elderly parents' demands, we get it done! We are so accustomed to taking care of everything and everyone. But we often don't care for ourselves and that is our biggest downfall.

There were moments when I had to ask God how I could accomplish everything I wanted to do with all that I already had on my plate. Having three kids, each in some type of after-school activity, as well as homework, cooking, and cleaning seemed like too much to handle. Then, finding the time to fit in accomplishing what I wanted was admittedly, difficult. Finally, one day, I reminded myself, "Remember, your journey is all about focusing on the circumstances you can change and not the circumstances you can't change." Once you allow the surroundings you can't change, stress you out, that's when you lose sight of what's important and give up your control.

At the time when I struggled financially, I made a choice to get assistance from the State to receive food stamps. Accepting that I couldn't afford to feed my kids was a hard reality that I had to face. I had to put my pride to the side and do what was best for my children. While getting help with groceries, I also took out a loan so I could attend barbering school. Going to barbering school allowed me to be a dual-licensed professional (Cosmetologist and Barber) and it allowed me to be able to service men and women. That one decision opened so many doors and gave me opportunities to increase my finances so I didn't need state assistance anymore. I chose to level up and get another license that set me apart from other cosmetologists.

172

I never gave up and because of my humility and determination, God blessed me financially for being faithful. I went from not having enough, to having just enough, to having more than enough. I went from public assistance to at one point making a six-figure salary. At one time, I couldn't afford to feed my children nor did I have enough money to keep the heat on during winter months; now I'm able to pay for international vacations along with my god-kids too. In order to find success, we have to get to a place where we learn how to work with what we have at the moment, while still working towards what we want for the future. If I had only focused on how other people excelled, I would not have reached the places I wanted to go. I had to understand that I still could achieve what I wanted with my career, I just had to take another route to get there. My journey was my journey and in order to succeed, I couldn't compare my journey to someone else's.

Being a woman of strength is about accepting where you are in life and who you are in life, then making the necessary adjustments and changes so you become the woman you desire to be in life. Stand strong and stand bold at the place you are in life right now, knowing that you won't always be there. You can create happiness in the midst of hardship by learning to believe that life will get better. If you believe, when you encounter hardship, that the moment is just another stop that you have to make on your journey, you can recognize that you won't be there long and your ship will continue to sail forward.

When I started walking in my truth, I started to make different choices. I started to really celebrate my mom's life. I looked at pictures of her again, telling my children her stories and taking them to her grave site. My son remembers my mother and even my daughters speak about my mother as if they met her before. They ask to go visit her grave to lay flowers there often; they always include her in their prayers or at family functions when they mention her and say I wish NaNa was here. The love they have for my mother is truly remarkable. I'll never forget the day my oldest daughter who was seven at the time, prayed at my mom's grave site. She said, "I can tell that you were a great mother because my mommy must get being a great mother from you." At that moment, with tears in my eyes, all I could think about was what my children would have missed, if I never made the choice to grieve and heal from her death. We all possess inner strength but we have to want to tap into that self-assurance so that we can overcome our circumstances. I made a choice to be strong, not only for myself, but also for my children, and most importantly to honor my mother's legacy. Our bodies aren't meant to stay here forever but the memories of our loved ones are what last a lifetime.

Being a woman of strength isn't measured by how many burdens you can carry, but by how you choose to put those burdens down and allow God to carry them for you. The strength of a woman has nothing to do with how much pain she can bear, but by how much happiness she can create for herself while bearing and healing from her pain. You have to start making you and your happiness a top priority in your life.

Take a moment to reflect and ask yourself, "How can I make adjustments in my life that will bring me some relief?" What burdens can you hand over to God so that you can free up your strength for you and your family?

There are certain areas in your life that you can't change but it's time that you take control over your thoughts and your reactions to those areas, even though you can't change them. As women, when you learn how to control your feelings and your emotions, you will start discovering how to control your reaction to life, even when it just isn't going the way you would like. You owe it to yourself to find the sense of peace that walking in your truth will bring to your life.

Remember, how you choose to treat yourself will always be the Standard of how you'll allow others to treat you.

Change Starts with You

Focus on you, make the necessary changes, then make yourself proud.

— Jenise McNair

It took a lot of pain, poor decisions, and disappointments before I finally realized that instead of trying to find the potential in a man who I thought needed to change, I just needed to focus on myself. It was easy to give others advice and encourage them to take control of their own lives but I wasn't taking my own advice and it clearly showed. We all have the ability to choose what we want out of life. Choose what's right, choose what's wrong, choose to give up, or choose to stay strong. At the end of the day, we make decisions that affect our lives, for better or for worse.

There will come a time in your life when you just get tired of being tired. You feel weary of being let down and disappointed. You must come to understand that you don't have any control over how others choose to treat you. Instead, you have all of the control of how you choose to treat yourself. When are you going to make the decision to change for the better? When are you going to stop ignoring that voice in your head that tells you, it's time for a change? Aren't you tired of that vicious cycle? That vicious cycle is *ruthless* and it's going to destroy you if you don't break out of it.

After two baby daddies and three children out of wedlock, I knew the time had come for me to change. There was no

176

way I was going to continue to make the same mistakes over and over again. My direction in life had to change and the only person who could make the necessary adjustments for change was me.

The first thing I did was ask God to help me. I started praying and reading my Bible more. I finally started being honest with myself. Most importantly, I began accepting and walking in my truth. Truth was, I was molested as a child. Truth was, I had premarital sex that caused me to have three children out of wedlock. Truth was, despite all my mistakes and poor decisions, I would not allow them to stop me from having God's best for my life. My past would not define who I was as a person or my worthiness as a woman. I understood that all I needed was to make a choice to want better. But not just want better, I had to make the choice to actually *do* better.

I allowed my daughters' father to make me feel insecure because I gained weight after having children. He used that leverage and called me fat when he got upset with me. I wouldn't have gotten upset if I was truly okay with myself and the size that I was, but truth be told, I wasn't okay. There's an old saying, "If you have a problem, then fix it." Well, that's just what I did. I started working on me from the inside out. I asked God to heal my wounds, forgive me for the mistakes I made, and help me to forgive myself. Most importantly, I asked God to help me forgive the ones who caused me pain.

It took me a long time to understand that forgiveness isn't for the other person; it's for you. Forgiveness allows you to completely be free so you don't let others actions alter your mood, feelings, or emotions. Without forgiveness, believe it or not, that person you have issues with will always have control over you. God helped me to learn how to forgive those who did wrong by me. It's not easy, but forgiving those who hurt you gives you such freedom, the result makes it all worth it. Learning to forgive those who hurt you is definitely a work in progress.

Ladies, regardless of the poor decisions you've made in life, you are still more than a conqueror and overcomer. But you must learn to forgive yourself to be completely whole. You have to understand that your mistakes in life do not depreciate your value nor your worth as a woman. Embracing who you are is accepting everything about yourself; the good, the bad, and the worst. Understand that you aren't perfect but also realize your flaws don't mean you don't deserve the best.

In order for me to change, I had to start taking a different action. I had to visualize myself going after goals that I always thought were impossible. I had to challenge myself to set goals and make sure that I finished what I started.

There's nothing greater than loving who you are and being content with being alone. That sense of fulfillment is what you call inner peace. When I experienced that peace for the first time, that calming feeling was something that I will never forget. For once, I wasn't worried about any of the situations that were going completely wrong at the time; instead I felt a sense of serenity as if I had everything under control. Having time alone with myself and God allowed me to rediscover who I was. I had a chance to find out what really made me happy about myself and what areas I wanted to improve. I've never been a weak person or a follower but I am still human and I fell short many times in my life. But I recognized my shortcomings could not be an excuse to continue to make poor decisions or fail in life. I had to create my own happiness in spite of the hardship that I faced.

One of the biggest lessons that I had to learn was only to focus on the areas that I was able to control and to pray about the situations that I couldn't. We spend too much time and energy focusing on the things that we can't control and we lose valuable time and energy we could use to invest in ourselves. The Serenity Prayer helped me to put my circumstances into perspective.

God grant me the serenity to accept the things I cannot change,

the courage to change the things I can,

and the wisdom to know the difference.

This prayer helped me really put my circumstances into perspective because no matter how much I loved my daughters' father, and wanted him to live up to his full potential, I had to understand that I couldn't make anyone do what they didn't want to do. Here I was, trying to help a man live up to his full potential, but I wasn't even focused on trying to live up to my own full potential. I put everything on the line for someone else's potential that I had no control over but wasn't doing anything to better myself.

Change happens when you *accept* the truth. I had to accept the fact that I couldn't change him into what I wanted him to be. But I did have the power and the ability to change myself into who I desired to be. The Serenity Prayer allowed me to accept and own the truth; and the truth is, you can't change anyone but *YOURSELF!*

Ladies, I want you to take a moment and repeat this prayer to yourself three times in a row. Let me tell you, that is a very powerful prayer because it causes you to reflect, to accept, and to make you want to change your circumstances. This prayer helped me overcome the trauma from my past. It helped me to understand even though some situations were out of my control, I still had the power to choose to overcome those traumas and turn them into triumphs.

Change truly starts with a choice and no one can make that choice for you. I was not happy with the extra weight that I picked up from my pregnancies but I realized I wasn't eating really healthy. The Serenity Prayer helped me realize this was an area in my life that I had full control over and could change. So, I contacted a good friend of mine who is a personal trainer. I told him I needed his help and how tired I was of being overweight. It was hard for me to find a babysitter so he came to my house twice a week for 45 minutes and helped me work out. The first day of working out, I felt like my heart was going to explode out of my chest. But rather than allowing that work to discourage me, I realized that I was in desperate need of a change.

Change truly starts when you get tired of running in that same circle operating in that same vicious cycle. Finally, you make a choice to take full control over your life. You begin to hold yourself accountable for every decision you make and take full responsibility over your life. No more excuses and no more complaining. Accept the things that you cannot alter and learn how to move forward while changing the things that you can. *Focus on you, create the necessary changes, and make yourself proud.*

My friend asked me what was my goal-weight. When I told him, he looked me in my eyes and said, "I'm going to get you there but you have to do your part." We made a goal for me to lose 25 pounds in three months which seemed impossible. But he believed in me so I had to believe in myself as well. I made a choice to work on the inside of me, my emotional, spiritual, and mental state, as well as the outside, physical state. So, there was no turning back. Losing weight requires a mental and emotional change. The first few weeks went by and I didn't lose any weight. I started to get discouraged but my friend told me to keep working hard and I would start to see results. I chose not to give up because I owed it to myself to remain committed and dedicated. If I could be faithful and constantly try to prove myself to a man who didn't treat me the way I deserved, then I knew I had to give myself what I deserved. I needed to keep going, no matter how hard it was to work out and eat right.

We are so anxious to see results right away, not understanding that everything worth having takes time. We are often impatient and that stops us from receiving what's meant to be ours. I continued to eat healthier meals and drink five bottles of water a day, even though I hated water. Fruit juice was my addiction. Previously, I drank about ten glasses of juice a day. But I learned that juice isn't anything but sugar and I realized sugar was the enemy of my plans to become healthier and my goal to lose 25 pounds.

As the weeks continued to go by, I finally started to see results. I looked in the mirror one morning and I couldn't believe that I had lost inches around my waist, even though the scale remained the same. Seeing the fruit of my hard work was an amazing feeling. I felt encouraged to continue my health journey. With dedication and determination, I lost 25 pounds in about three months. I was the smallest I had been in a long time and I looked amazing for my sister's wedding. Hard work truly pays off! The only step I had to take was to make the choice to change and follow through with that decision.

I was on cloud nine after losing 25 pounds and I actually felt happy about myself again. I had three kids yet I looked pretty darn good. That's when I realized, change truly starts within us. Change starts when you choose to put yourself first and really desire something better. You are the only person who can make a choice to change and meet the expectations you hold for yourself. You have to be the one to make a decision to change and believe you have what it takes to make the necessary alterations. No matter how fat I felt, how insecure I was when I looked in the mirror, or how my stomach disgusted me, only I could make the choice to do something about my weight.

Change is very hard; it's actually one of the greatest challenges in life. As adults, we are especially tested because we have already formed habits that are difficult to break. When we make a choice to change, we open the door to discomfort, for sure. Change brings the new and unfamiliar, and it takes you out of your comfort zone. But more importantly, we have to focus on the fact that change can be good. We change elements in our lives every single day because most of the areas that we adjust or rearrange are easy for us to do. Altering ourselves as a whole or trying to break a bad habit, that's when change becomes very difficult. Some change takes little to no effort but other changes require hard work.

Change only happens when you are tired of being stuck in a vicious cycle and you are honestly ready for something different. Change happens when you are ready to take accountability for your life. Change starts with you and your mentality because the body follows the mind. If we feel mentally content where we are physically in life, then content is just what we will be. In life, we become mentally tired before we are physically worn down. The body can't stay where the mind has moved from. We have to stop running or giving up just because new challenges cause us to feel uncomfortable. Look, if you want to become the best version of yourself then "Get comfortable being uncomfortable!" Understand that being content and comfortable doesn't allow room for you to grow.

My weight-loss journey didn't stop there; my health success made me want to change other areas of my life. Every day, I tried to figure out what other places in my life I needed to work on. I felt like I needed to challenge myself more; I needed to dig deep and really push myself past my limit. We don't know what we are capable of accomplishing until we make a choice to try. After finding success with my health, I decided to run a half marathon. My older brother completed one so he inspired me to go outside of my comfort zone and challenge myself in a big way. Twenty-six miles seemed impossible, especially since the most I ran previously was two miles. I decided the first step toward this challenging goal was to do a half marathon.

When I went to support my brother during his full marathon, I saw men and women twice my age running the distance. I thought to myself, "Now what's my excuse? I won't know if I can really become a runner if I don't make the decision to try." So that's what I did; I didn't just talk about running a half marathon, I actually made a choice to start training for the race. With three kids and two jobs, I had to figure out how to make time to train but this challenge was something I felt like I needed to do, so I made time for it. I continued to train twice a week with my trainer and I ran three or four times a week on my own. I went from running one mile to five, then from five miles to eight miles. Every day I set a distance goal and every day, I told myself I wasn't coming back into the house until I finished.

Finally, the day of the race came, but the farthest I ran before the race was 10 miles. I was nervous, and scared of how I was going to compete, yet I knew that I owed it to myself to fight and push through to that finish line. I hoped to see my brother before the race because he was my comfort and inspiration through my whole training process, but he was late so I didn't get a chance to see him. I felt nervous because I was worried that my legs would cramp up early in the race. As a runner there's good days and then there are bad days and I just hoped that day my legs were going to have a good day!

The race started and with three miles in, my legs felt pretty strong. I had my headphones in my ears as I ran, but I felt somebody creep into my personal space. They didn't move past me so I finally looked up and guess who it was? My brother! I gasped with joy. He ran almost three miles full-speed just to catch up with me. He helped me to relax and took my focus off monitoring how my legs felt. We talked, we laughed, and he made sure I crossed that finish line like a *Champion!* As I crossed that finish line, I felt so relieved. I worked hard for that feeling of accomplishment and no one could take that from me, not even the devil.

She Believed She Could So She Did — Unknown

The truth is, I lost 25 pounds, I ran a half-marathon, and yet I still yearned for more. I was so shocked by my accomplishments that I wanted to challenge myself even more. I really enjoyed that feeling of setting a goal and successfully accomplishing that goal. The discipline that it took to train honestly made me a better person and made me even more disciplined with my eating habits. I couldn't just stop there; I wanted and needed more of a challenge. I learned truths about myself that I never realized before. So right after the race, I told my brother I was going to continue training and run a full marathon. All 26.2 miles!

This moment is when I knew training was going to get real for me. Deciding to train for a full marathon had everything to do with my mental commitment to train and run longer miles consistently. Training and running daily really put the areas of life that I seemed to struggle navigating through into perspective for me. Some days I felt good and some days I felt bad, but regardless of how I felt, I knew I had to keep pushing forward. What seemed hard for me one day only became easier for me over time.

Training for a full marathon was really a big deal, especially after hearing horror stories from other people who ran one before. Some people told me that they would never run a marathon again, while other people said it was an experience of a lifetime. I am the type of person who

185

needs to meet challenges for myself and actually go through the process. Someone else's experiences may be different than yours so it's good to be open to trying new things yourself. I needed to stretch my mind even more, knowing I had to train my body to be able to conquer 26.2 miles. I knew this commitment was bigger than just getting in physical shape. Training for this full marathon required a mental commitment that no matter how tough it got, giving up wasn't an option!

When I trained for my half marathon, my brother was my encourager. I felt like I needed his support and presence for every run, no matter how many miles I ran. But I knew this time around, I needed to conquer the obstacle alone. And I learned that it is acceptable to face challenges alone. Every day, before I went out for a run, I asked God to give me the strength to finish my run, even when I felt like giving up. Training for the full marathon taught me so much; every mile I ran prepared me for the next mile.

Life causes us to experience disappointments that we didn't plan on but we must learn how to push forward and keep going. Our life's agenda isn't always going to go the way we planned but that does not give us an excuse to stop pushing forward toward our goals. I discovered that running is more of a mental battle than a physical one. There were days when I planned to run eight miles, but as soon as I started running, I felt uncomfortable. Immediately, I started to think, "If I'm already feeling uncomfortable at mile one, how in the world am I going to finish eight miles today?" I realized that I had to keep running and keep pushing, even through my discomfort. The body truly follows the mind which means once you've made your mind up, the body has to follow. "Mind over matter" means how your body feels at the moment, doesn't matter when you've made your mind up to continue to push forward.

Every time something new makes us feel uncomfortable, we automatically want to stop and give up but we can't. We have to learn how to push through the apprehension or distress. Your new direction doesn't even have to pertain to working out. Public speaking is also something that causes a lot of people to feel uncomfortable. It takes someone who's not used to speaking in front of a crowd out of their comfort zone. When I ran, even though my legs felt uncomfortable at the beginning, as I continued to run, I started to feel better. And the next thing you know, I completed eight miles. The first sign of discomfort isn't an indicator to stop or give up; discomfort can simply be an opportunity for you to grow. Mental toughness will always outweigh our physical capabilities. Even though my legs at one point were in pain, I just encouraged myself not to stop and to continue to run through my discomfort.

As I continued to stretch my comfort zone, the time came when I had to run farther than what I thought I could do. In order to prepare for the marathon, I had to do 14, 16, or 18 miles which seemed incredibly far to me. I had to remind myself that the way I was going to run those longer distances was the same way I reached 13 miles. I set a finishing goal and did not come back into the house until that goal was completed.

Change doesn't begin with the physical aspect of yourself, it starts with your mental thought process. You will never truly be able to change until you've mentally accepted that you *need* to change and that you will do whatever is necessary to change. We can want so many features in life but the question is, do we really take the necessary steps to get what we truly want out of life? Do we take action? Change is not easy, but it is definitely worth the sacrifice, especially if that change is going to cause you to become a better version of yourself. Change takes a lot of effort, determination, self-motivation, and dedication.

If you never learn how to fully commit to yourself, you'll never learn how to fully commit to anything.

Change will allow you to tap into your mental capabilities, move past your mental barriers, and utilize your no-limitations thought process. You must believe that there isn't anything you can't achieve once you've made your mind up that you're going to achieve it. Again, the body will always follow your mind's thinking. Whatever it is that you believe or tell yourself usually comes to pass over time. When we are hungry, we instantly think about what we have a taste for. Then we think of a place to eat and most of the time you end up choosing that place for dinner. The mind is a powerful tool that we often misuse; yet our mind gives us the ability to choose what we want out of life. No matter what life presents in front of you, when you make up your mind to go after your goals and dreams, nothing will be able to stand in your way.

I achieved a goal that I never thought I could accomplish. I trained and finished my first full marathon. All 26.2 miles. It was a feeling that was indescribable. On the day of the race, I told myself, "I don't care how uncomfortable or painful my legs may feel, I'm going to do whatever it takes to cross that finish line." I'll never forget the memory of seeing my children running toward me as I approached the end of the race. Tears welled up in my eyes as I said to myself, "Wow, you believed you could finish and you actually did it!" That moment made me realize nothing was impossible to those who believe in themselves.

Accomplishing that goal and completing a full marathon was one of the best feelings I ever experienced in my life. I lived my life, selling myself short all this time, not knowing what I was fully capable of. After completing my full marathon, I wondered how I could hold myself accountable every year and challenge myself to continue to grow physically and mentally. I truly enjoyed how running made me feel and how it caused me to have time to meditate on the things that I wanted for myself, my children, and my future. Running for hours caused me to have to think about many areas of my life. When I was outside running, I had nothing but time to gather my thoughts.

When I decided to change for the better, I knew that I didn't want to change for just that moment in time. I wanted to try to become the best version of myself that I could possibly be. I didn't want my change to only last for a moment. I wanted the changes I made to be consistent in my everyday life. To make sure that I held myself accountable and continued to challenge myself as a whole, I decided to run a full marathon every year.

Temporary change takes place when you choose to change for others; but permanent change only happens when you choose to change for yourself.

Training for a marathon each year allows me to be disciplined by having a training schedule and sticking to it. I also have to be disciplined with my food choices. Training for marathons also helped me to mentally prepare to go after my other dreams and aspirations that I once thought were too big or impossible. I strive to keep the same mindset of dedication and commitment, no matter how difficult the process gets. While training, every minute of my day is accounted for and I always work to be productive, without wasting any time. I normally start my training after my birthday in mid-February, all the way until October when I compete. I enjoy how I feel mentally and physically during my training season because I am constantly working out and processing all the important concerns that are on my mind at that moment.

Running causes me to always challenge myself and focus on becoming a better person. Running is humbling on numerous levels because even when I don't feel good running, I've learned to push through that discomfort to achieve great endeavors. *As you grow, so will your vision.*

We can't always be comfortable in life; there will be times when you will feel uncomfortable and you must learn how to adapt. I'm not saying you need to become a runner like I did in order for you to change for the better. But running has truly helped me to make those uncomfortable changes comfortable. You also need to find whatever it is that will challenge you mentally and physically. Remember your main focus should be to make sure you are as healthy as you can possibly be, physically and mentally. No, you don't have to become a runner but incorporating an exercise plan should definitely be a part of your daily routine. In the beginning, you may feel sluggish and try to make up fifty excuses on why you shouldn't work out. But as soon as you complete your workout, you will feel amazing and you will be so glad you exercised. There is a mental challenge when it comes down to being consistent in your routine, even when your body doesn't want to cooperate. But when you make up your mind to commit to yourself and your goal, perseverance will see you through.

We know change isn't easy but it's for the best in most situations. There's no growth without change! I honestly never thought I could become the person that I am today. I waited until I was almost thirty years old to really know what it feels like to push myself past my limits. I wish I had this mindset when I was younger but I'm also glad I have this mindset now that I am a mother of three. I was an athlete in high school and I played basketball most of my life. But looking back on how I trained and played in high school, I now wonder if I truly gave my all and played hard enough.

Now that I am grown and a mother of three, I continue to play an ongoing game of one-on-one with this thing called life. A lot of my shots were blocked, a lot of shots were missed, and I even had some bumps and bruises because no fouls were called. It really has been one heck of a game but through every failed attempt, I learned how to take the lead and win. Tough times truly cause you to tap into your inner strength and use a part of yourself you never had to access before. I know it's difficult for you to look up and you see everyone around you passing you by but you can find a way to catch up and surpass them. In order to make that happen, you have to readjust your life plan and do something different. Don't let what you've done in the past hold you back.

Ladies, when you are tired of being in a relationship that doesn't bring you happiness, your first thought is that you're ready to leave. You might not physically leave the relationship right away but mentally, you've already left. The body follows the mind, so once you've mentally reached the desire to leave a relationship, the body will soon follow. When you are mentally tired of being where you are in life, that's when you make a plan in your mind and physically make an effort to change and take action.

We get so caught up in everything and everyone around us, that we only become interested in trying to change those around us instead of just trying to change ourselves. In my past relationships, I always tried to improve the guys I dated, to help them reach their 'full potential.' Once I went through the process of trying to change myself and seeing how hard it was to adapt to new circumstances, I realized that I was completely out of mind believing I could change a grown human being who didn't want to change in the first place. I put so much effort, time, and energy into others yet they had no intention to try and become better. Now that I think back to those moments, I was clearly wasting my precious time because I didn't understand that I had no control over anyone but myself.

Your father won't become a better father until he makes a decision that he wants to do so. The father of your children won't become a better co-parent until he chooses to do so. And you won't become a better mother until you make a decision to always do what's best for your child no matter how you may feel. You can't control the choices of others; you have control over you and only you.

Every single day you have a choice to become a better version of yourself. You have a choice to eat better or go to the gym. You have a choice to tell yourself to stop smoking or drinking so much; stop cursing and yelling every time you get upset. You are in control of you and the things you choose to do in life. But you have to figure out what is most important to you: the temporary pleasure you want now or the future dreams you want most. Whatever you want the most will definitely cost you your time, your effort, and your energy.

When making a choice to change for the better, the process is what shapes you and molds you. The process is what builds you up and holds you accountable. The process allows you to appreciate the different phases of growth you go through. The process is what helps you become the woman you are meant to be.

First you have to evolve, then you'll become.

I came to a place in my life where I started going after the goals that were once impossible to me. I evolved into a woman who refused to accept less than what I deserved; even from myself. Running marathons only made me *Dream Bigger*. It made me want more for myself out of life and now I'm willing to do whatever it takes to get there. I can't tell you how drastically my life changed since I made a decision to only focus on what I wanted most in my life and the areas that I knew that I could change. I am a five-time marathoner because I chose to focus on myself. Running marathons was the start of me becoming the best version of myself and going after everything I set out to do in life. Most importantly, that choice made me hold myself accountable and prioritize my life to put myself first. I believe it's time that you make a choice to do the same.

Don't sell yourself short because you keep expecting others to give you what you can give yourself. You must ask yourself if changing in a way that provides you a better life is worth your time and effort. Change doesn't happen overnight. Every goal we set will always consist of a process and trusting that action. Right now, you must make a choice to want better and do better. I'm challenging you to start making a change today, no matter how little or big the improvement is. The most important part is your decision to at least try. Change challenges you but it always makes you better. Make a choice to change, accept that it will be uncomfortable and mentally prepare yourself to push through no matter what, until the end.

You are worth giving yourself the very best version of yourself!

Remember, how you choose to treat yourself will always be the Standard of how you'll allow others to treat you.

Conclusion: Potential of Man

"When I see potential I just gotta see it through."

— Drake

There is potential in each and every one of us. Potential to be who we've always wanted to become and potential to do what we've always dreamed of doing. Potential causes us to make certain decisions based off what we would like to happen, but the reality of the matter is that Potential is what *could* be yet there's a strong possibility that dream may *never* be.

There are a lot of times in life when we don't take our circumstances at face value. We are very selective when it comes to what we want to see and who we want to listen to when it comes to dating, especially when we receive information we aren't ready to accept. When we see potential in a man, we think we just hit the jackpot. Potential leads and guides us to a world full of possibilities, but what we fail to realize is that potential and effort go hand-in-hand. I can honestly say I never made an effort to live up to my potential until I made a choice to change, at the point when I felt down and out.

I was a woman who was hurting, broken, and completely lost. I allowed myself to continue to go through the same vicious cycle, year after year. Putting all of my time and energy into someone else made me lose sight of my own identity. For years I tried to help my man reach his potential while I drowned in my own pain and sorrow from my past. But then the pain I felt from carrying so many burdens became too much to bear. All the love that I tried to pour into him, I should have poured into myself. Think about how much effort we put into these relationships especially the relationship where you'll be the only one making the effort. We go above and beyond trying to build a man up and we don't put any of that effort into ourselves.

As women, we never take the time to properly heal before we make a choice to move forward. We have to learn how to sit in our pain, learn from our pain, and heal from our pain. Ladies, I know how you feel; I know what you're going through and I'm telling you don't have to stay in that space. You don't have to remain somewhere you don't want to be. You don't have to continue the same vicious cycle you keep repeating year after year.

Growing up, I had so many unrealized capabilities until I learned how to activate my potential and started to reach for it in every aspect of my life. I made a choice to go after the impossible. I sought after happiness that was beyond my circumstances at the moment. I followed God and the joy that I knew only He could give me. I envisioned myself facing challenges that most people wouldn't expect a mother of three to be able to do. I thought bigger than my circumstances; I wanted more for myself than I ever desired before. Most importantly, I made a choice to properly treat my past wounds that I covered with temporary band-aids, simply because I didn't want to deal with the pain. Making a decision to walk in my truth allowed me to accept the circumstances in my life that I couldn't change and make an effort to work on the things in my life that I could change.

Walking in your truth at first, may be one of the hardest things you've ever had to do. But I promise you, honesty is one of the best gifts you could ever give to yourself. I used to think traveling the world wasn't an option for me because I would never be able to afford it. I thought my dream vacation was always going to be just that; my dream vacation. Despite my financial hardship, I was determined to become a world traveler. I realized nothing was impossible for me to do and I started to believe in the potential that I had inside of me. Learning to be disciplined and not spending unnecessary money allowed me to see that traveling the world was possible and reasonable. More often than not, when we think something is impossible, we don't even try to find ways to make it possible. I made adjustments with my thought process and how I chose to spend my money. Traveling was possible when I stopped eating out and buying shoes that I didn't need. I started to be frugal and disciplined with the little bit of money I had and then God started blessing me with little increases year after year.

I changed my mindset and it changed my life. I've never really been a disciplined person but I had the potential to be disciplined. When I started making an effort that's when I started living up to my potential. I began to travel and I finally had my dream vacation and so much more; I visited South Africa, Egypt, Jerusalem, Turkey, Canada, London, St. Lucia, St. Martin, Cuba, Costa Rica and many more places. Believe it or not, I never even paid for any of those trips on a credit card either. Because I found my potential, I overcame the statistics of single mothers being broke and struggling. I no longer allowed myself to live in a box of impossibilities but instead, I chose to go wherever I envisioned myself going and to do whatever I envisioned myself doing.

When we don't know who we are or what we want, we subject ourselves to settle for far less than what we deserve. When I believed I deserved the *best*, that's when I started getting the best and living my best life. I know what it's like to be at the lowest point of your life; better days seem nearly impossible and so very far away. But you have to ask yourself at that moment, are you really taking the time to focus on yourself, to live up to your own potential, to be the best woman that you can possibly be?

Men aren't the only ones who need to live up to their full potential; women need to make an effort to live up to our full potential as well. I believe the world would be a better place if everyone really just focused on themselves and made the effort to live up to their full potential and really made the choice to become the best version of themselves. There's potential in every person that walks this earth but it is solely our responsibility to live up to that promise; financially, physically, spiritually, mentally, and emotionally.

There will never come a time when you reach a point in your life and believe you can't better yourself, no matter what age you reach. There isn't one perfect person in this world which means there is always room for growth in each one of us. We never stop learning which is why we always learn something new about ourselves when we challenge ourselves and make the effort to try.

How do we learn to maximize the full potential in ourselves? Without effort, potential really holds no value, yet we make a lot of life-altering decisions based off potential. We have no control over the potential that someone else may possess, we only have control over the potential that we possess inside ourselves. The action that we put behind our potential is the effort that we make to see our potential through.

Potential causes us to believe, to be hopeful, to have something to look forward to. But in reality, potential has to be driven by action in order for it to hold any kind of weight. We give potential too much credit and imagine it to be more than what it is. Everyone has the potential to be whoever and whatever they would like to be but they must want to reach that possibility and be willing to take the necessary steps to achieve it.

It is so important to take the time out to really examine ourselves and learn who we are even before we tap into the potential we possess inside. Learning who we are, the good and the bad, allows us to be transparent with ourselves and make adjustments accordingly. True self-evaluation allows us to understand the areas we need to change about ourselves and the places that can remain the same. If we don't take the time to get to know who we are from the inside out, we will never be able to maximize our full potential. We will continue to allow others to dictate our lives.

If you can't acknowledge or accept the areas of your life that you need to work on, how will you ever overcome those areas that may hold you back from achieving your goals? When you truly take the time out to get to know yourself, you are able to acknowledge the good, the bad, and the ugly; that's when you can finally start the process of living up to the full potential that God intended for you to live.

I was my first life-coach client and I was able to be honest and take self-criticism from myself, as well as self-encouragement. No one knows you better than yourself; no one knows your fears but you. No one feels your pain and trauma but you. No one can overcome your circumstances in life but you and no one keeps you from being great but you. So, I coached myself through the hardship I was going through. I coached myself through my healing process to become whole. I realized that I would never be successful as a Life Coach if I didn't learn how to help myself first. I found the solution to my problems and the solution to the problems that many other women face as well.

Walking in your truth is the solution to having the life you've always dreamed of living. Having the confidence to know exactly who you are, your purpose, and your self-worth will encourage you to no longer settle for anything less than what you deserve. Walking in your truth empowers you to create happiness for yourself that no one can ever take away. You are the only one in control of your happiness. Walking in your truth will give you a sense of security that enables you to feel okay with being alone. It will allow you to be patient and stop you from rushing into a relationship that was never meant for you.

I was once broken financially, broken emotionally, and a complete mess with no direction on where to go. Change is very hard but trying to change someone else is even harder, almost impossible. I've always wanted to help people or make whatever problem they had go away. During my past relationships, I sacrificed my happiness trying to help men find their true happiness. I wanted to give all that I could in a relationship, to help them forget about any disappointments or trauma they had experienced in the past before we started dating. I wanted to love them past their pain but the problem was they couldn't love me in return until they learned to love themselves first. How does a woman who goes out her way to bring happiness to others only end up hurt in the end? Because that woman never took the necessary steps to deal with her own past pain; she didn't even know how to bring inner happiness to herself.

Understand, you can't live through others, you can only live through yourself. I was that woman who tried to help others, thinking that was going to mend my own brokenness. You can't effectively help other people until you learn how to help yourself first. I learned a tough and painful lesson the hard way but it was a lesson that was needed. I discovered how to offer help that won't compromise my own happiness. I have a passion to help others but I had to learn that helping others truly started with learning how to help myself first. Again, no one knows your life, your struggles, your fears, or your shortcomings better than you. Being transparent and honest with yourself will allow you to grow and blossom into the woman you are meant to become.

Every story that I wrote about in this book, I experienced and lived through. I'm so confident that you can overcome anything and everything you are facing and can live the life you've always imagined because I did it for myself. Focusing only on myself and the situations that I could change transformed my life forever. God allowed me to go through my circumstances so that now I can be a resource to women around the world. Not everyone knows where to start or how to make a change but if you don't take action or choose to put yourself first, you will continue that same vicious cycle that you find yourself in year after year.

You owe it to yourself to finally put you first and to start walking in your truth. It's time to hold yourself accountable and take ownership; do something different because you've held yourself back for far too long already. You are worth going after all of your dreams and aspirations. Don't ever apologize for attempting to do so. I know it's easier said than done, which is why my purpose is to be a resource to women across the world and help women start their journey of choosing themselves first and really experiencing true happiness and joy!

If you would like to talk to me in person and chat about the start of your new journey of putting yourself first, I would love to help you! Go here to tell me more about yourself and set up a free call to take the first steps toward changing your life: https://www.FreeHerTruths.com/book

There's potential in each of us but living up to it solely depends on us as individuals. Just imagine being free, creating the life you've always wanted, truly having inner peace and joy, and obtaining all the dreams you once thought you could never have. We normally fail ourselves by continuously making the same decisions that aren't in our best interests. Trust God and know He will never fail you. God gives us the ability and free will to make our own choices. So, do something different this time. Make a choice and choose you!

There's no need to wait any longer, I believe in you and I believe you want the best for you too. If you don't remember anything else from this book just remember this: How you choose to treat yourself will always be the Standard of how you'll allow others to treat you!

"Embrace who you were, Embrace who you are and Embrace everything you are Becoming…"

About the Author

Jenise is an Entrepreneur, a Certified Life Coach, and a Motivational Speaker with a powerful message that demonstrates how you can achieve the unthinkable while overcoming obstacles and doing the impossible. Her message is straightforward: "Stop expecting others to give you what you can give yourself." When Jenise applied that simple message to her own life, she transformed for the best. Jenise makes an effort to go after all of the things that were once impossible to her. She is now a five-time marathoner and an inspiration to women across the world.

Jenise has been a licensed Cosmetologist for 16 years, a licensed Barber for six years and a Cosmetology Educator for ten years. She always had a passion to help others and she used her talents and gifts to make others feel good about themselves. Jenise also used teaching as a way to give back. She encouraged her students to push forward and to go after all of their dreams and aspirations. Her students inspired Jenise to continue to follow her dreams as well.

Jenise McNair is a natural motivator. She encourages and inspires women to push forward in life, despite the obstacles that arise during many phases in life. Her story of transformation is proof of the principles she uses to empower women. She believes that when you mentally challenge yourself and choose to be better, nothing can stop you from getting the best out of life.

Jenise has overcome sexual abuse, domestic violence, financial hardship, and her own personal insecurities that held her back from living up to her full potential. She now travels extensively throughout the world, hoping her story will inspire women to never give up and to become the women they are meant to be.

Jenise lives in Largo, Maryland and is the mother of three amazing children, Jelani, Jaylah, and Jordyn. She learned how to overcome adversity by developing mental fortitude and beating all the odds set to prevent her growth as a woman and mother. She believes your circumstances in life are only permanent when you choose to accept them as defeat. She believes you are only as Great as you think you are. So, don't just think you're Great, know you're Great!

If you feel inspired to face your truth and be free to live the life you deserve, Jenise would love to hear from you. Find out more at www.FreeHerTruths.com or follow her on Instagram: @woman_of_strength31.